WALLED GARDENS
OF SUFFOLK

SUFFOLK GARDENS TRUST

© Suffolk Gardens Trust, 2014

All Rights Reserved. Except as permitted under current legislation no part of this work may be photocopied, stored in a retrieval system, published, performed in public, adapted, broadcast, transmitted, recorded or reproduced in any form or by any means, without the prior permission of the copyright owner

First published 2014

ISBN: 978-0-9931470-0-5

A CIP catalogue record for this book is available from the British Library

Published by Suffolk Gardens Trust

PHOTOGRAPH CREDITS
Front cover: Parham Hall walled garden courtesy of Juliette Wade
Back cover: Thornham Hall walled garden © Tina Ranft
Title page: Langham Hall, entrance gates and pavillion © J. A. Broster
Page iii: Chilton Hall, the exterior wall © Tina Ranft
Page iv: Somerleyton Hall, inside one of the peach houses © Tina Ranft
Page 1: Abbot's Hall, lean-to glasshouse in the walled garden © Tina Ranft

Designed and typeset by Tina Ranft

Printed in Great Britain by
The Lavenham Press Ltd
Tel: 01787 247436
enquires@lavenhamgroup.co.uk
www.lavenhampress.com

www.suffolkgardenstrust.org

CONTENTS

Editors' Preface: How this book came to be written	iv
Suffolk Gardens Trust	vi
Acknowledgements	vii
Foreword	ix

FEATURES OF SUFFOLK WALLED GARDENS

Introduction	1
The Position and Shape of Walled Gardens	4
The Walls	8
Water	13
Glass	16
Buildings	20

CASE STUDIES

Abbot's Hall, Stowmarket	27
Barton Mere House, Great Barton	31
Langham Hall, Langham	34
Nowton Park, Bury St Edmunds	38
Rendlesham Hall, Rendlesham	42
Tendring Hall, Stoke-by-Nayland	47
The Walled Garden, Horringer Manor, Horringer	51
Woodside, Constitution Hill, Ipswich	54
Case Studies: Endnotes	57
List of Suffolk Walled Gardens	60
Glossary of Walled Garden Terms	64
Select Bibliography	69

EDITORS' PREFACE

How this book came to be written

Arriving at this point has been a long and rewarding journey and there was a point where we, the Walled Garden Group, realised that we would never exhaustively record all the county's walled gardens, but needed to make a record of how far we had got to enable others to continue. In the first place Suffolk Gardens Trust (SGT) realised that many walled gardens were falling into decay and it was necessary to record them before they disappeared altogether. To recruit and train a group, a study day was organised by James Carr, Adam Paul, Patricia Shepherd and Polly Burns at Hengrave Hall in the back sheds of its walled garden. We are delighted that Susan Campbell has agreed to write a foreword, as she was our keynote speaker at that initial study day and she was the person that enthused us to the point that has kept us going for nine years. Sixteen people signed up at that initial study day.

Over the years many have contributed and stayed a while, but the following have all been involved in the production of this book, Adam Paul, who was Vice Chairman of SGT at the time and had restored his own walled garden at Parham Hall and, in alphabetical order, Margaret and Michael Bampton, Diane Boyd, Jenny and Tony Broster, Polly Burns, Tim Heath, Harriet Holt, Tina Ranft and Nigel Surry.

One of our problems in producing this book was that we decided early on that we would survey the walled gardens in winter, it might have been cold and wet, but at least we were not bothered by nettles etc. in the more derelict gardens, and we were not in danger of ruining crops in the productive gardens. The downside to this is that many photographs are very wintery and bleak and we have had to work hard to find some 'pretties' to enliven the book!

In terms of how we went about surveying the walled gardens, we prepared a list of ones we knew about, appealed to members for suggestions, which were excellent and were frequently augmented by new suggestions. At a later date, when we hoped to produce a definitive list of walled gardens we went through the Ordinance Survey (OS) maps held by the Record Office. This was a most interesting exercise, until we realised that from our practical experience, many of the smaller or irregularly shaped gardens could not be identified accurately from the scale of the maps. It has to be said that around Newmarket the studs and training establishments were a further source of confusion!

For each garden to be surveyed, OS maps are produced and distributed to the group, along with preliminary notes to provide background plus a check list survey form, before we wrapped up well against the weather and sallied forth to survey the garden in question. Reports were then prepared with additional research from the Record Office, before being distributed among the group for comment and criticism, and finally a copy was sent to the garden's owner. Additional, less obvious research tools such as using a metal detector at Abbot's Hall and in two instances, referring evidence of daffodils to the now retired RHS Daffodil Registrar, SGT member, Sally Kington.

We appreciate that the convention is to use wholly metric measurements, but in the case of walled gardens we decided that as they were constructed in imperial measurements, it would be easier to visualise and more meaningful to provide both imperial and metric measurements.

In particular we would like to thank Jenny Broster who has generously allowed us to use her thesis as the basis for the section discussing the component elements of walled gardens. Saying that reminds us that we have been able to help other students with their projects and thesis, thereby realising one of the Garden Trust movement's aims to help the younger generation to appreciate and understand our landscape history and heritage.

We all would like to thank the Suffolk Gardens Trust Council for their constant support, both in terms of morale and latterly financial and The Stanley Smith (UK) Horticultural Trust, The Alfred Williams Charitable Trust and The Scarfe Trust for generously sponsoring us so that we have been able to produce a book whose price we hope will be within everyone's reach.

We hope this book will inform and enthuse readers and that they will want to find out more about this specialised aspect of our landscape heritage. However, we want to stress that there is not necessarily an unrestricted or restricted public right of access and would ask that any reader wishing to visit any site mentioned should contact Sufffolk Gardens Trust in the first instance, or consult the Tourist Office or the current NGS 'Yellow Book'. Punctuation and spelling have been standardised throughout the text of this book.

Polly Burns, Tina Ranft and Nigel Surry

SUFFOLK GARDENS TRUST

Promoting, Recording, Conserving, Enjoying
All Aspects of Gardening and Landscape in Suffolk

The Suffolk Gardens Trust was founded in 1994 as a result of a rising interest in, and concern for, the county's gardens and gardening heritage.

Gardens have many levels of interest – as works of art; as historical or archaeological records; as sites of architectural, horticultural or scientifific significance; through associations with notable people; or as important sources of spiritual and sensual enjoyment.

Many of Suffolk's gardens are internationally famous and attract thousands of visitors each year. Some are secure in the ownership of organisations like The National Trust or through the committed stewardship of their private owners, but others are vulnerable to decay, unsympathetic alteration and even total destruction. Suffolk Gardens Trust champions the care, conservation and recording of the county's gardens.

THE AIMS OF THE TRUST ARE

- To stimulate an appreciation of Suffolk's gardens through visits, talks and publications
- To compile a register of Suffolk gardens
- To promote the study and recording of Suffolk's gardens – their history, designs, plants and tools
- To promote and encourage the care and conservation of Suffolk's gardens

BENEFITS OF MEMBERSHIP

- A newsletter twice a year
- Visits to gardens that are often not normally open to the public
- Lectures and seminars on gardening topics
- Opportunities to take part in garden history research
- Opportunities to take part in surveying and the recording of gardens
- Opportunities to meet people with similar interests

For more information please visit www.suffolkgardenstrust.org

ACKNOWLEDGEMENTS

The Suffolk Gardens Trust would like to thank the following for their support: St. Edmundsbury Council; Suffolk County Council; Suffolk Libraries and Suffolk Record Office. Suffolk Records Society gave permission to quote from N. Scarfe (ed. and trans.), *A Frenchman's Year In Suffolk: French Impressions of Suffolk Life in 1784*, Suffolk Records Society XXX (Woodbridge, 1988), p.3, and Blackie & Co allowed us to quote from Julian Trevelyan's *Suffolk Scene* (London & Glasgow,1939), p.11.

We are grateful to all those garden owners who allowed us to undertake surveys, particularly those who lent us documents and other records, namely: Karen Angell Dancer, Diana Blackwell, Emma Dowley, Jim and Marion Mountain, the late Brian Phillips and Susan and Christian Stenderup.

Isabel Ashton, Susan Campbell, James Carr, Karen De Rosa, the late Fiona Grant, Sally Kington, Roger Last, Edward and Joanna Martin, Paul Miles, Uhi Millington, Phil Mizen, Lucy Spofforth, John Smithson, Professor Tom Williamson, Juliette Wade and Hector Wykes-Sneyd, are among the many individuals to whom we are indebted.

Nor do we overlook the contribution by the following County Gardens Trusts: Devon, Hereford and Worcester, Isle of Wight, Norfolk, Staffordshire and Warwickshire.

Generous grants from The Stanley Smith (UK) Horticultural Trust, The Alfred Williams Charitable Trust and The Scarfe Trust have enabled us to keep our costs at a level that ensures the book has prospects of far greater circulation than would otherwise have been the case.

The progress of this work has not been without its moments of gloom and anxiety, in which the encouragement of our patron, The Lady Marlesford, together with that of our Council and its Chairman, Stephen Beaumont, have proved vital to its eventual appearance.

Polly Burns, Tina Ranft and Nigel Surry

The walled garden at Ashe Park, now filled with flowers.
© *Tina Ranft*

FOREWORD

I am so pleased (and also rather proud) to learn that my visit to Hengrave Hall in 2004, to speak at the Suffolk Gardens Trust's walled kitchen garden study day has succeeded not only in keeping its research team going for the past 10 years, but has resulted in the production of this most impressive book.

My archive shows that I took some 15 slides of Hengrave's kitchen garden on that occasion, the highlight being the discovery of a glasshouse incorporating patent glazing by Beard's of Bury St Edmunds. This was the first time I had ever seen an example of Beard's glazing, and I well remember the slight puzzlement of the group that had invited me, over my excitement. But it was a real pleasure to be able to tell them that they had a bit of valuable horticultural history there, and that it was precisely such remnants of the past that made the preservation and research of old walled kitchen gardens so worthwhile and important.

Even so, the recognition of that importance has still some distance to go. It is all the more rewarding therefore, that the Suffolk Gardens Trust has undertaken and completed such a useful survey of their own walled kitchen gardens and that, as I write, they have their counterparts in two other County Gardens Trusts, with Oxfordshire and the Isle of Wight.

It is no easy task to recruit and train sufficient volunteers to undertake the work required for a proper survey of any type of garden, let alone walled kitchen gardens, where so much of the knowledge of how they functioned in their distant heydays has been lost. But for me the unearthing of that past has been, for the past 35 years, incredibly rewarding, and I am just so chuffed that the interest and enthusiasm is, it seems, on the increase. This can only be good news for the preservation, re-use and appreciation of these wonderful old gardens, and I congratulate the SGT on their enterprise in producing this book.

Susan Campbell

The grand entrance to the moated walled garden at Helmingham Hall.
© *Edward Martin*

FEATURES OF SUFFOLK WALLED GARDENS

INTRODUCTION

The Suffolk landscape 'has a wonderful variety ..., not only in crops ... and in the texture of the soil, but in its intrinsic make up as well. We have river, valley, corn, plough, pasture, moor, marsh, wood, heath and sea-shore. Can the restless mind or the most difficult taste demand more than these?' These words of Julian Tennyson's ring as true today as when written in the 1930s, although much has changed. The clay lands of central or High Suffolk have lost much of their woodland to fields of prairie-like proportion, while in contrast a great deal of the coastal strip or Sandlings together with Breckland are given over to the coniferous plantations of the Forestry Commission, and the Fenland has been drained and is now intensively farmed. Many – but not all – of the walled gardens surveyed by Suffolk Gardens Trust belonged to the mansions grouped around Bury St Edmunds or Ipswich, and along the route of the A12 – the edge of the Sandlings. This is a landscape not only shaped and modified by geology, but also by its economic and social history, which is clearly reflected in the siting of 200 or more walled gardens belonging to country estates, farms, parsonages and market towns that are recorded for posterity on the 1st and 2nd editions of the 25 inch to a mile Ordnance Survey maps of the 1880s and 1900s. However, it is sad that very little photographic evidence remains of these gardens in their heyday.

Productive gardens in the sixteenth and seventeenth centuries varied in size from 1 to 4 acres (0.404 to 1.618 hectares) and were often just one group of walled compartments near the house. Their position meant that produce had only a short journey to the kitchen or flower-arranging bench. Being close to the stables, it was easy to transfer dung, used as manure in the garden, into the walled compartments. François de la Rochefoucauld, writing in the 1780s, described the gardens he had seen – mainly around Bury St Edmunds – as 'so extremely small compared with ours, not more than four or five arpents (an arpent varied between a half and five sixths of an acre), even for bigger houses. The vegetables are very well cultivated, mostly in heated glasshouses, which are common in England: I can't speak as to the noblemen, but certainly for the ordinary gentry, indeed I've seen them in the majority of town gardens'. An inventory of 1723 reveals that almonds, mulberries, peaches and cherries were then grown at Glemham Hall, and a more detailed list of fruit, vegetables and flowers drawn up some ninety years later gives oranges, peas, hollyhocks, roses, potatoes, cabbages and raspberry canes – an indication of the extensive range of plants available at this period.

Though this gives the impression that walled gardens were the larders of great country houses and their owners' town houses, many were very modest gardens attached to rectories, such as Drinkstone and Grundisburgh. In both cases there is no evidence to suggest that there were glasshouses, substantial service buildings or even accommodation, though without boilers to be stoked continuously to heat glasshouses, and as they were situated in villages where the gardeners were likely to live, most service buildings and accommodation would be unnecessary. Yet the gardens of the gentry were, at times, remote from their houses – some designed to be visited by owners and their guests, notably at Thornham Hall and Horringer Manor. In the latter case, paths led through the pleasure grounds, and down and across the walled garden, leaving via an ornate gate and bridge over a stream that was dammed to form a canal. The earliest gardens, such as those at Chilton and Kentwell, were designed to be ornamental – part of the pleasure grounds and productive – and in both cases the garden slopes down to a moat that forms the fourth enclosing side of the garden. This leads us to the arcane question as to what is a walled garden? In this book we have taken it to mean a garden producing flowers, fruit and vegetables for the house. In the case of Woodside in Victorian Ipswich, the garden is walled on only two sides, with the natural topography forming the other two enclosing elements. However, within its L-shape there is every feature that one would expect in a garden supplying a comfortably off middle class family.

Glemham Hall was not alone in the opportunities it offered to gardeners. At the turn of the century an impressive range of fruit and vegetables was grown at Benacre Hall, in a walled garden of 2 acres (0.81 hectares), including five varieties of peach, six plums, three cherries, two apricots, five pears, seventeen apples, twelve gooseberries and four kinds of strawberry. The two vineries held four and five distinctive vines, there were two peach houses and an orchard house with apples, figs and peaches in pots. And there was also room for potatoes, onions, sea kale, salsify and endives for the family and its guests. On her first visit to Barton Hall in 1824, Lady Bunbury was 'delighted to find a garden ready walled, quite sufficiently large both for flowers and kitchen garden and well adapted for these purposes'. It was *c.* 3 acres (1.81 hectares) in extent and was soon to be planted with peaches, nectarines, pears and apples. In contrast, the Reverend Arthur Ashton, Rector of Uggeshall, abandoned his vinery in favour of fruit and flowers, achieving fame for a particular variety of primrose. Ashton was content with his one glasshouse, but in the gardens of the wealthier gentry there was an impressive growth in the number and variety of such structures. Saxham Hall, with a walled garden of 2.5 acres (1.01 hectares), boasted two melon or cucumber houses, two orchid or plant houses, a conservatory, two peach houses, a vinery and two cold houses. Peter Grieve, head gardener at Culford Hall (1847–1880), 'planned and laid out the principal kitchen garden of eight or nine acres' [and], it was said, 'as a successful cultivator of flowers, fruit and vegetables, Mr Grieve has few equals and no superiors'. At the height of his career, Grieve presided over a garden with three orchid houses, with peaches, nectarines, cherries and figs in a vinery, peach house, fig house, melon house and cucumber house. Nowton Park (formerly Nowton Court) became well known for its numerous species of pears. However, at Ashe High House, Campsea Ash, by 1914 the old kitchen garden was 'now given up to flowers'. This was unusual for kitchen gardens. Both large and small gardens mostly continued to produce fruit and vegetables for the family and their guests, selling off any surplus when the opportunity occurred, as at Livermere Park where in 1899 the sale of fruit and vegetables brought in £50 a year.

Maintenance and running costs of such gardens varied considerably. J. H. P. Oakes, MP for Bury St Edmunds, rebuilt the walled garden at Nowton Park between 1875 and 1878 at a cost of some £10,000 to £11,000. Clearly, enterprises on this scale were only for the wealthy and ambitious when staffing considerations are also born in mind. The 14 acres (5.67 hectares) of gardens – including the kitchen garden – at Livermere were under the care of a head gardener and five under-gardeners, assisted by an old man and a boy, at a cost of £292 a year. But at Redisham Hall at the time of the 1925 sale it was claimed that 'the upkeep is very modest, the grounds 2 acres (0.81 hectares) at present thoroughly well maintained by two men and a boy'. Head gardeners were paid as much as £100 a year, and on larger estates staffing levels were extremely high. At Shrubland Hall in the 1860s, apart from the head gardener, there were three under-gardeners, twenty-five labourers and seven boys, as well as a plumber, carpenter and carpenter's boy, all paid from the garden account.

It was not only owners such as Sir Richard Wallace at Sudbourne – who built conservatories and vineries and extended the kitchen gardens – whose money drove these changes, but also developments in garden technology in which Suffolk played an important part. Ransomes of Ipswich, established in 1783 and famous for their agricultural machinery, developed a profitable line in lawnmowers by the 1860s. In the same decade Charles Beard, a horticultural engineer at Bury St Edmunds, patented and sold his Glass Wall – thin sheets of rough plate glass bolted onto iron frames, designed with the protection of walled fruit trees in mind. By the 1880s their contemporary Boulton & Paul of Norwich was not only producing lawnmowers, but also glasshouses, boilers, garden rollers, wire, watering cans and tools of all kinds that were sold on a national and international scale.

The Great Depression of the 1880s, together with the impact of World War I, brought widespread social and economic change, hastening the decay of the great estates and a more general crisis in the countryside, with an inevitable impact on walled gardens. The break-up of estates, often accompanied by the demolition of the house to which their fortunes were tied, led to further sales, fragmentation and even neglect. Some mansions, for example Sudbourne Hall and Rendlesham Hall, suffered greatly at the hands of allied troops during World War II, and the mansions were subsequently demolished and their gardens left to decay. More were eventually lost to housing development, as at Easton Park and Great Barton, while at Hintlesham Hall – now a hotel – much of the walled garden is now a car park for a newly-built golf club, with the remainder being the site for a private house and its garden.

A major problem hindering restoration of walled gardens is the sheer cost. Yet despite this some have been more fortunate. The walled gardens of the Benhall Lodge estate were bought in 1926 and transformed into a viable commercial nursery that continues to flourish; the kitchen gardens at Brent Eleigh Hall and Woolverstone Hall were for a period run as businesses. A ten-year restoration programme at Thornham Hall – completed in 2000 – allows the walled kitchen garden to be run as a charity for training the disabled in horticulture, while at Redisham the Hall and gardens are now successfully managed as a family trust.

In recent years there has been a resurgence of interest nationally that can perhaps be said to have been led by Tim Smit, with the restoration of the productive gardens at Heligan in Cornwall. The National Trust have recently begun the restoration of the walled garden at Ickworth Park in Suffolk, English Heritage have carried out impressive work in the kitchen garden at Audley End in Essex, while a new Suffolk walled kitchen garden was created at Cobbs Hall, Great Saxham in the early years of this century. A popular interest in organic fruit and vegetables has encouraged some owners or tenants to exploit the possibilities of their own gardens, with well-established box schemes at Langham Hall and Livermere Park, while the Walled Kitchen Gardens Network encourages a countrywide interest in their future.

We can now look more closely at key factors or elements determining the function of walled gardens.

THE POSITION AND SHAPE OF WALLED GARDENS

The position of the walled kitchen garden in relation to the house is interesting because it gives an indication of the age of the garden. Until the seventeenth century it was generally situated within easy reach of the house. With the advent of the landscaped park in the eighteenth century it was not thought desirable to see any type of garden from the house windows and so the productive garden was relocated further away, thus requiring a carriage drive or leisurely stroll to be taken by the family if they wished to inspect the garden. This was not always the retrograde step it may appear. With hindsight the new position could have advantages, such as increased size and a slope towards the south, with the result that the garden would be in the sun for longer during the day and that frost would drain out more easily. The new site may also have had more fertile well-drained soil. Smells coming from the large quantities of dung used as fertilizer were a further practical reason for putting distance between the house and the kitchen garden.

The kitchen gardens created from the mid- to late-nineteenth century were normally more closely integrated with the pleasure grounds and ornamental gardens, and so by implication they were positioned further away from the house. This is illustrated by the close position of older walled gardens to their mansions, such as Hintlesham Hall, Benhall Lodge and Glemham House, whilst later nineteenth century gardens such as Bawdsey Manor and Nowton Park are further away.

In Suffolk it was often the case that the garden was moved when the house was rebuilt. When Somerleyton Hall was rebuilt in the 1840s the gardens were repositioned at the same time – away from the house to the opposite side of the pleasure grounds and then subsequently grassed over. At Ickworth the house was rebuilt but the walled garden remained in its original position close to the site of the old house. However, not all gardens were moved away from the 'big' house. By 1723, Hintlesham Hall had a group of enclosures nearby – in a similar fashion to Somerleyton – and the kitchen garden appears to have been one of these enclosures. The walls of the garden at Hintlesham can still be seen – situated near the stables – where they were in 1883, and it appears they have remained in the same place since at least the early-eighteenth century. In March 1821 the Rev. Thomas Mills of Stutton visited the Misses Lloyd at Hintlesham and commented that, 'the Grounds are flat but the elder Miss Lloyd is a great Florist and the Gardens are really well stocked'. They were still productive in 1948, but have since been laid mainly to tarmac. Some of the newer Suffolk walled gardens remained in their original position as they were never part of a cluster of walled compartments near the house. The gardens at Bawdsey Manor and Benhall Lodge (now The Walled Garden, Benhall) are two of these.

Bawdsey Manor gardens were laid out between 1885 and 1909. The only features in the area on the 1843 tithe map are the site of a Martello Tower and a small farm complex that later became the estate's dairy. The kitchen garden is first shown on the 1903 Ordnance Survey map and lies approximately 164.01 yards (150 metres) north-east of the manor house (Fig. 1). The garden designers Parsons, Partridge and Tudway have been credited with the design of the kitchen garden, which included a central lily pond, shrub borders and wide grass paths in addition to fruit and vegetables. Between the productive garden and the mansion are two pleasure gardens, one of which lies on the site of the Martello Tower. The kitchen garden was some distance from the house and it was not so conveniently situated to easily transport dung from the farm.

Older than Bawdsey Manor, the walled garden at Benhall Lodge is

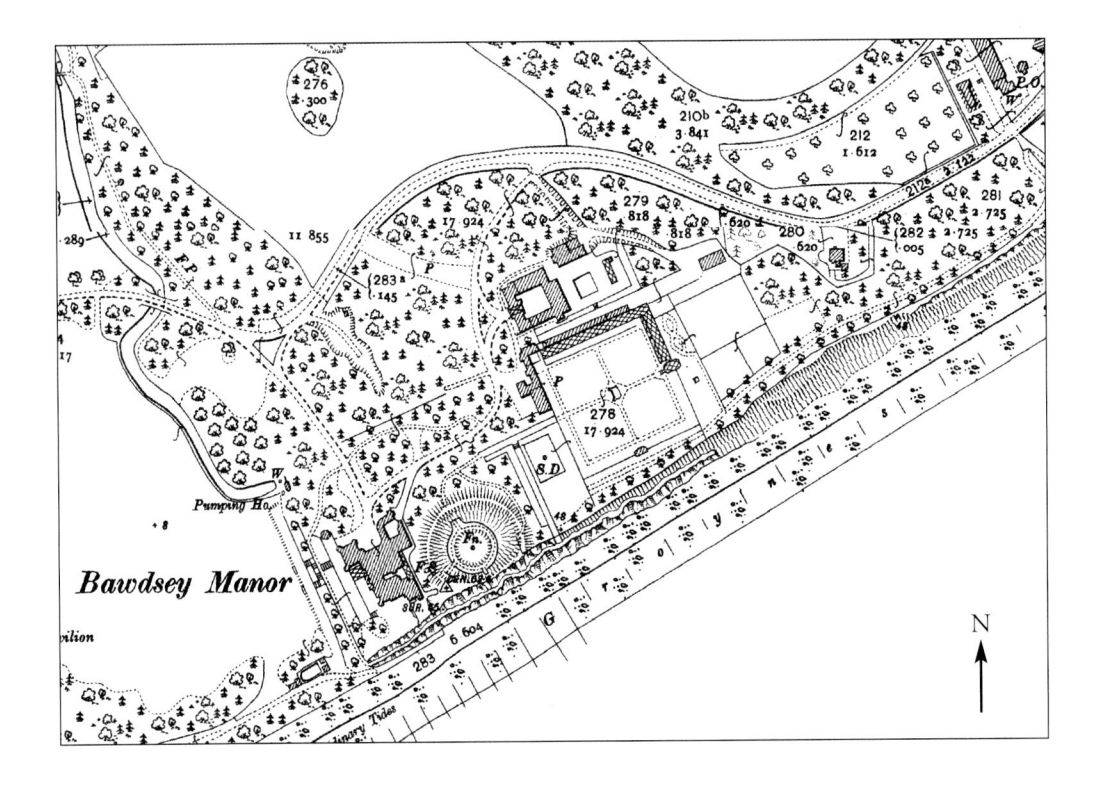

Fig. 1: Bawdsey Manor as shown on the 1903 OS map. The kitchen garden is the square-shaped feature (centre), with pleasure gardens separating it from the mansion to the south-west. From OS Map 2nd series, 1903. Courtesy of Ordnance Survey

thought to have been built at the same time as the new house c. 1815. The Rev. Thomas Mills visited Mr Holland at Benhall in January 1819 and commented on 'a most capital Kitchen Garden'. It is shown on an estate sale map of 1830 and is in the same position as it is today, c. 200 yards (182.9 metres) to the north and slightly to the west of the house, whereas at Bawdsey the walled kitchen garden is over five times that distance from the house. Perhaps it was felt unnecessary to site the walled garden a long way from the house at Benhall because it was screened by trees. Although screening appears to have been attempted at Bawdsey, the sunken garden and the low-lying area of the second pleasure grounds would have made it difficult to provide an effective screen for a productive garden nearer the house.

Glemham House also has a walled kitchen garden that has remained in the same position since its inception. It lies to the north of the house – adjacent to the stable block – in a position that is reminiscent of Somerleyton's gardens in 1663. This may be due to its age, although dating this garden is particularly difficult. Sale particulars dated 1829 include the kitchen garden to the north, containing cross paths that met at an ornamental basin. The house was completed in 1818 by the architect Thomas Hopper for the Rev. Dr. Samuel Kilderbee, and it is thought that the kitchen garden was created at the same time as the rest of the park, before the house was constructed. If this is correct, the garden could have been built as early as 1811. The present owner, Lady Cranbrook, says that it has been productively 'in use continuously since Regency times', which would support this.

Most, but not all, walled gardens built in Suffolk during the eighteenth and nineteenth centuries were either square or rectangular. However, there are exceptions with examples where the square or rectangle shape is slanted by lengthening opposite walls to expose the maximum amount of wall to the warmth of the sun. Opinion was divided as to whether orientation should be inclined towards the east, west or south. J. C. Loudon took the view that east was better because it caught the morning sun. Horringer Manor walled garden is sited this way. At Parham Hall the slant is to the west, illustrating the alternative theory that the afternoon sun was warmer and persisted later in the day, allowing the wall to retain the heat into the night. In addition, this orientation meant that blossom was not damaged by a sudden thaw in the early morning sun.

In some gardens the design took on a more complex shape. At Glemham House the north wall is polygonal. Although unusual this is not unique, especially given the garden's estimated age. Nationally, Repton built several six- or seven-sided walled gardens in the 1790s, including Broke Hall's kite-shaped garden. Other similarly shaped gardens in Suffolk are at Orwell Park, Brettenham Hall, Coldham Hall and Rougham Hall. The most irregular is the six-sided garden at Barton House, where it is thought that the south-east facing wall was extended and pushed out to form a curve that gave greater exposure to the sun. The resulting narrow south wall created a small area that was used as a site for the palm house, with a subdividing wall behind it to conceal the working garden. Similarly, triangular-shaped gardens with the northern angle sliced to form a trapezium can be found at Boulge Hall, Culford Hall and Ickworth. There has to be a degree of caution in assuming that these unusual designs were created solely to maximise exposure to the sun, because topography would also have been a consideration. Nevertheless, the importance of a warm, south-facing wall for fruit growing cannot be underestimated. There were other ways to increase the available area of south-facing walls – subdivision, or the creation of a garden within a garden, was one technique used in Suffolk. Benhall and Thornham walled gardens are examples of subdivision, whereas Langham Hall has walled compartments within the garden. At Benhall the tithe map of 1847 shows a building running east to west across the centre of the rectangular site, with a gap at either end leaving room for easy access to both halves. At Nowton Park the dividing range, which was built between 1876 and 1885, divides into thirds – one third to the north and two thirds to the south, with space at both the west and east ends for access.

As stated above, the majority of gardens were rectangular or square and divided into four compartments with axial paths. Each section was edged to prevent soil falling onto the paths and thus degrading the hoggin from which they were usually made. A wide variety of materials were used for edging, ranging from live edgings of box or herbs to hard edgings made of planks of wood, purpose-made tiles or low wattle fencing. Paths were also protected by using boot scrapers that were situated at the corners of each bed so that gardeners could clean their boots before walking on the paths.

THE WALLS

Walls are the essential element of any walled garden. Not only do they lend their name to the subject, they also visually identify the garden as a separate unit. They are there not merely as boundaries but as part of the design to increase the productivity of the garden. The walls provide a microclimate that benefits the produce that is grown in the open ground of the garden, as well as acting as warm supports to fruit trees planted against them. In addition, they form a barrier to deter predators and thieves. The material used to construct them depends on what is available locally.

Suffolk has very little natural stone and a surfeit of clay, so bricks were in use from as early as the twelfth century. As an attempt to recoup some of the cost of the American War of Independence a brick tax was introduced by Pitt the Younger in 1784, which made bricks very expensive. Just before the tax was repealed in 1850, fifteen per cent of the cost of a good quality brick was attributable to the tax. However, because the tax was levied per brick, the cost was reduced by increasing their thickness, so that fewer were needed for a given area of wall. The average size of a brick in 1729 – regulated by a statute of that year – was 8¾ x 4⅛ x 2½ inches (22.23 x 11.43 x 6.35 centimetres). This increased to 10 x 5 x 3 inches (25.4 x 12.7 x 7.62 centimetres) after 1784. By the time the tax was repealed brick kiln technology had improved, and these two factors combined to make bricks more affordable. Where there was a brick kiln on or near the site of a walled garden – as at Benhall Lodge, which produced an estimated 300,000 red bricks – there were no transport costs involved and so the walls were far less expensive to construct. Thornham Hall also had its own kiln, and it is estimated that the bricks in the walls there date from *c.* 1700. It is believed that over-burnt bricks (overburns) were exempt from tax, and it is noticeable that they are frequently incorporated into the walls of walled gardens, sometimes – as at Glemham Hall – in an attractive diaper pattern.

Because of its strength and its ability to absorb heat during the day that was then released slowly as the air temperature cooled at night, brick was the material of choice for walls wherever possible. This meant that Mediterranean fruit ripened far more easily. Nails, to support fruit or restraining wires and other devices to train fruit, could easily be knocked into a completed brick wall. In many gardens these characteristics were further exploited by using the outer and inner sides of the walls and the

Fig. 2: Serpentine or crinkle-crankle dividing wall at Heveningham Hall. © Tina Ranft

ground at their base for additional planting. This was especially prevalent on those walls facing east, west and south. Those on the outer walls were known as slip gardens and were used for hardy fruit and vegetables that needed space – but not much cosseting – or to duplicate planting of a crop that was growing inside the walls in a less favourable position so that the crop would be retarded and the season extended. This system and layout are clearly visible in the walled gardens at Horringer Manor, Saxham Hall and Glemham Hall.

Serpentine or 'crinkle-crankle' walls were a way to economise on the number of bricks used to build an enclosure wall because they only required a thickness of one brick, whereas a straight brick wall needed at least two, depending on its height. They were particularly prevalent while the brick tax was in force. Given the cost of bricks and the scarcity of a good alternative material, in addition to the close proximity of the Netherlands – where the design is thought to have originated – it should, perhaps, be of no surprise that there are more examples of serpentine walls in Suffolk and Norfolk than in the rest of the country. A list of these walls – compiled before 1993 – estimates that there were (allegedly) ninety-two surviving serpentine walls in Suffolk at that time. Some are to be found at Coney Weston Hall, Easton Hall, Heveningham Hall (Fig. 2), Melford Hall and Parham Hall. A less well-known example is at Rendlesham Hall where the undulations are notably less curved than is common, so much so that from a distance the 6 feet 6 inches (1.98 metre) high wall appears to be straight. Part of it has collapsed and another section has been reinforced with slim buttresses extending to the top of the wall and centred on each of the undulations. Rendlesham also incorporated serpentine in older parts of wall, contrasting with later nineteenth-century wall construction. That reinforcement was necessary is not surprising on a wall of that height that

Fig. 3: Part of the remaining section of serpentine wall at Easton showing its single brick construction.
© J. A. Broster

is constructed at single brick thickness, and with little curvature to stabilise it (Fig. 3). Theoretically, a serpentine wall should, in effect, have buttressed itself to give greater stability, but over time the poorly designed serpentine style proved to be a false economy.

Apart from being less expensive, the very shape of serpentine walls was said to produce sheltered alcoves for fruit and also a greater surface area of wall over an equal distance. However, there was some debate as to how much of an advantage the alcoves gave fruit grown within them. Certainly, Loudon was of the opinion that the shelter the alcoves provided was 'generally denied by practical men', but Susan Campbell has pointed out that 'although the curves acted as sun traps for fruit, those same curves were thought to cause the wind to eddy, thus injuring the trees'.

The height of the walls was relative to the size of the garden, and this usually varied between 10 to 19 feet (3 to 6 metres). They needed to be of a sufficient height and strength to provide the protection and support necessary to grow sturdy plants. The larger the garden, the taller the walls could be to give maximum protection before their height would restrict sunlight falling on the productive body of the garden. Tall, long walls needed supporting buttresses or piers along their length to prevent collapse. Usually these would be on the outside of the garden where they would not reduce the area available for training fruit.

There are examples where the walls in an individual garden vary in height. Brent Eleigh Hall is one such: here the eastern wall is 15 feet (4.57 metres) high and the north wall 10 feet 3 inches (3.12 metres), while the southernmost wall is 5 feet 1 inch (1.55 metres) tall. The western wall – which has internal buttresses – varies in height along its length from 10 feet (3.05 metres) at the northern end to 8 feet 6 inches (2.59 metres) at the southern end. Thus, because it slopes quite steeply from east to west, it is the topography that necessitates the differing heights of three of the walls. However, the low south wall in relation to the higher north is not unusual, as this arrangement allowed maximum light to strike the south-facing side of the north wall. At The Walled Garden, Benhall, the change of wall height is for a different reason. Here the north wall is higher at its eastern end. This is because it once formed the fourth wall of sheds, and the boiler house behind it, that stood outside the garden. Similarly, at Woodside in Ipswich, a section of the north wall has been raised to accommodate a glasshouse that hangs off it. Other gardens where walls have been raised in height to accommodate a glasshouse can be seen at Chantry Park in Ipswich, Glemham Hall and Bawdsey Manor, where the wall behind the elaborate lemonry is higher than the rest of the east wall.

With any wall it is essential that the top edge is protected from rain, which would otherwise seep into it and cause deterioration. There are three main methods of creating a protective edge along the top of a brick wall: capping bricks, coping bricks and brick-on-edge coping. The coping brick is formed so that its projecting ends throw rain clear of the wall, whereas a capping brick has no such projection and relies entirely on its shape to disperse water. Half-round coping is a common shape and can be found at Brent Eleigh Hall. Stone was a more expensive material than brick and was most often used on the walls nearest the house for its visual effect, as at Bawdsey Manor and Tendring Hall. There is an interesting variation on the third protective method – brick-on-edge coping – at Hintlesham Hall. Here the topmost course of protective brick surmounts a further course of shaped bricks, under which there is a projecting layer of headers and stretchers. These act as a support to the shaped-brick course above, and also as coping bricks by encouraging rain to fall well clear of the wall (Fig. 4). Studying them in more detail, it can be seen that the two bricks were joined to form a near triangular shape, with the right angles joined at the top of the wall. The bricks laid on edge would protect this joint. A further variation of the brick-on-edge coping arrangement can be seen at Langham Hall, where there is a drip line of slate below the protruding layer (Fig. 5).

Walls constructed of a mixture of brick and local flint can to be seen in parts of Suffolk, although they do not last as long as those made entirely of brick. At Horringer Manor walled garden the west and north walls are built of red brick. In contrast, the south wall, which is constructed of brick and flint, is in poor condition and bowed. The walls at the Old Rectory, Drinkstone are mainly of flint rubble with brick pillars, and knapped flints and chunks of brick are also present in the east wall. The brick pillars appear to have strengthened the walls in general terms, although they have been breached in one area. Perhaps flint – a readily available material in some

Fig. 4 (top): Shaped bricks on the top of the wall at Hintlesham Hall.
© J. A. Broster

Fig. 5 (above): Drip line of slate below protruding layer of brick on the west wall at Langham Hall. The slate may also have prevented water seeping into the bricks below.
© J. A. Broster

FEATURES: THE WALLS

parts of Suffolk – was used alongside brick to reduce costs. At Barton Mere two of the less visible walls are made from a variety of materials – an eclectic and eccentric mix of brick, flint, tiles and even glass bottles – that are not laid in courses, but seemingly thrown together. It is unclear if this was to reduce costs or due to eccentricity on the part of the person who built the wall.

High, long walls not only provided protection from the weather, but also acted as a deterrent against the theft of produce and implements. Separate entrances were required for the family and workers. Occasionally there was an additional entrance for the head gardener, as at Glemham House. At Thornham, Nowton and Horringer it is notable that gates used by the family are far more imposing and ornate than those used by staff, and at Horringer Manor they are part of the overall design and integration of pleasure grounds and productive garden, whilst the series of ornate gates are effective in draining frost from this sloping garden. Paradoxically, walled gardens are designed to provide a sheltered micro-climate, but where they are on sloping sites frost can get trapped and roll down to the lowest level, with potentially damaging results. There is an aperture in a wall at the foot of the sloping walled garden at Tendring Hall that appears to serve no obvious functional purpose other than to drain away the frost as it rolled down the slope. However, the aperture is at the point nearest to the estate farm, so it could have been a convenient place to take manure from the stockyards into the garden.

The element of security provided by walls is well illustrated at Broke Hall. Records show how many gate keys there were and also their distribution among the garden staff, suggesting that security was an important issue. The head gardener had a master key to fit all the glasshouses, the conservatory and plant house, as well as the kitchen wall and flower garden gates. The peach, pine and vine houses had the same key, although this was a different key from the others. The same criteria applied to keys for the orchard, fig, and cucumber houses and also the long range. Unique keys were provided for the banana and fruit houses.

Technology in the late eighteenth and nineteenth centuries enabled the development of hot walls. These required a wider wall and more bricks than a conventional brick wall, but the result was additional heat that helped tender fruit to ripen. Hot walls were created by running horizontal, internal flues across the back of the wall, which opened into chimneys at the top of the wall. Fireplaces were placed at the rear of the wall in line with its foundations. There is evidence of a hot wall at Benhall, although remaining pipework indicates that technology had moved on in the twenty years or so from 1790 to *c.* 1815, which is the estimated date of the garden's creation. Smoke had been replaced by water and the fireplaces had been replaced with boilers – much of the south-facing wall had been heated by water that moved around by convection, running through 4-inch (10cm) cast iron pipes from three boilers. The system must have been successful, because the south-facing wall has a numerous holes made by the nails that held carefully trained fruit trees, indicating the *raison d'être* of the heated wall. According to a sale catalogue dated November 1832, Langham Hall also had hot walls in its kitchen garden for forcing fruit.

WATER

A water supply has always been fundamental to the success of a productive garden. Eastern England is the driest part of the country with an average rainfall similar to that of Israel, so extensive and inventive methods of water storage have always been used in Suffolk walled gardens. By the mid nineteenth century water was used not merely for watering plants, but was also needed for pipes that heated glasshouses and used for cleaning produce and equipment. Probably the oldest method of storing water is in a dipping pond. Dipping ponds have been in use since the fourteenth century. As the name suggests, water had to be scooped out of them by hand using a watering can or something similar. Traditionally, they were shallow with a thick clay lining that was protected by stones or gravel. Frequently, they were the main central focal point and sited where the paths dividing a walled garden into quarters met. Good examples can be found at Glemham House and Sudbourne Hall. In the case of Sudbourne, the 1904 Ordnance Survey map clearly places the dipping pond in the centre of the rectangular garden, though a second dipping pond was found outside the walls that would have serviced a further range of glasshouses. Water carriers (known as water engines by the Victorians) were used to transport water from the dipping pond to wherever it was needed. Glemham House still has a water engine, although it is unclear whether it is still used for its original purpose (Fig. 6). Another example is to be found at Barton Mere House. Despite advances in hydraulic technology that would logically have made them obsolete, dipping ponds were still being constructed in eighteenth- and nineteenth-century gardens. For example, a large part of the walled garden at Sudbourne Hall is thought to have been developed as late as the 1870s, and yet dipping ponds were still part of the layout (Fig. 7).

Reservoirs or tanks were also

Fig. 6: Water engine or carrier at Glemham House. © J. A. Broster

Fig. 7: Dipping pond at Sudbourne.
© *J. A. Broster*

used for storing water – the terms cistern, reservoir and tank all signify a container rather than a pond or pool that occurs naturally. These containers could be found above or below ground, and most were covered to avoid evaporation. Before the advent of pumps it was important that the tank was on higher ground than the garden, thus giving sufficient flow of water to the garden below, where taps were used to release it as needed. Where the topography does not lend itself to producing sufficient flow – as is often the case in Suffolk – water-filled barrels were dragged from the storage tank, either by man or horse. A more sophisticated solution was used at Tendring Hall, where its sloping location allowed water to be pumped by wheel from a well sunk into a stream. From here it was stored in a tank at the top of the mansion, from where it was distributed to smaller tanks around the site. Laid out *c.* 1776, Woolverstone Hall walled garden had a lined irrigation reservoir and four water tanks, while Woodside employed both static and portable tanks (Figs. 8 and 9), some of which had slate covers to prevent water evaporation. Slate was also used to form water tanks and examples have been found at Horringer Manor and Abbots Hall.

In the 1860s pumps were introduced, enabling water to be extracted from below ground or moved across ground, thus eliminating the need for portable carriers. Joseph Evans & Sons of Wolverhampton was founded in 1810 and manufactured a variety of pumps. It carried a lion rampant trademark from the 1890s, and a number of pumps with this trademark can be found at Carlton Hall, near Saxmundham. At Benhall and Horringer House walled gardens the water was pumped to storage tanks in glasshouses – Benhall's water coming from nearby ponds, whilst Horringer House's water was raised from a well within the garden. The pump at Langham Hall is recorded on the 1884 Ordnance Survey map and was used to raise water from a well of considerable depth. A tank is still visible under the floor of a storage shed in a complex of buildings that included bothy and potting sheds, and a further galvanised tank collects water from the surrounding roofs. A number of pumps at Saxham Hall were fed from water collected in the adjoining laundry, but also from a stream that had been diverted to flow under the walled garden. Here, pumps are shown on the Ordnance Survey map of 1884, notably at strategic points where more water would have been required, and thus requiring less labour than was needed with older-style dipping ponds.

It was not until the end of the nineteenth century that reservoirs and water towers began to be supplied with mains water. A red brick water tower was built between 1886 and 1904 at Woolverstone Hall. Although the tank itself is now missing, the pipes descending from it were still visible in 2005. It is not clear whether the water was forced to the top of the tower by a ram, or whether the new technology of using pressurized mains water was available.

Fig. 8 (above): Galvanised tank in glasshouse at Woodside. © J. A. Broster
Fig. 9 (below): Portable water tank at Woodside. © J. A. Broster

GLASS

Fig. 10: Ridge and furrow glazed roof glasshouse at Somerleyton.
© Tina Ranft

During the nineteenth century many factors contributed to the dramatic rise in the use of glass in the kitchen garden. Firstly, the glass tax was repealed in 1845. The high price had hitherto severely restricted its horticultural use for all but the wealthiest, but when glass prices dropped – by as much as eighty per cent following the tax's abolition – glass became more affordable. Secondly, the technical advances of the industrial revolution also accounted for the rapid increase in the area put under glass. As a result of improvements in the manufacture of cylinder glass by James Hartley in 1847, clearer and larger panes that transmitted more light could be produced. Thirdly, new designs for glazing bars – both cast iron and wood – were also developed around this time. Later, in 1871, Loudon is credited with the invention of the ridge and furrow roof, although it was Joseph Paxton who first put this system into practice. These allowed more of the sun's rays to enter the glasshouse earlier and later in the day than had previously been the case with flat lean-to glasshouses. In addition, the undulations of glass had a filtering effect on the more extreme heat at midday. There is an excellent example of a ridge and furrow glazed roof at Somerleyton Hall (Fig. 10). Rendlesham Hall once had a variety of glasshouses and stove houses, both inside and outside its walled garden, which were all dedicated to fruit and flowers. The peach and the fig were popular in the nineteenth century, but it was the pineapple and grape that really became fashionable and thus encouraged the use of more glass.

The pineapple craze took hold in the eighteenth century, maintaining its popularity with the wealthy until mid-Victorian times, when pineapples started to be grown by the middle classes. On large estates growing orchids replaced the pineapple in importance. Pineapples do not grow to a great height so could be grown in a pit. These were usually in the frame-yard or forcing ground – so called because the glass casements (or 'lights') that were used to support insulating straw mats looked very similar to window frames. Over time the whole structure – including the bed – became known as a frame, regardless of what material was used to form its walls, which could be brick or stone, but was usually wood. These frames were originally placed in open ground – often close to the stables, which provided dung as the source of heat. The use of dung or manure was superseded by the development of boiler systems. In the mid nineteenth century, frame yards were usually sited closer to the glasshouses where they could benefit from their hot water systems. These manure-heated systems can be identified by low arches, through which copious amounts of manure were shovelled. Notable surviving examples in Suffolk can be found at Liveremere Park, Glemham Hall and Hintlesham Hall.

The use of frames was widespread in Suffolk. At Langham Hall an inventory of 1832 refers to 'one cucumber double-frame single ditto and light' and at Ashe High House, Campsea Ash, sales particulars dated 1883 mention 'a Twelve-light Range of forcing Pits' as well as 'Ranges of Marrow Pits'. The 1934 sales details of Sudbourne Hall refer to 'a range of heated pits' and Rendlesham Hall's 'complement of glass' included two melon pits and cold frames'. In the slip garden at Glemham House a disused melon pit survives, and rectangular-shaped foundations – including a brick arch to allow the insertion of dung or manure – have been found in the overgrown frame yard at Hintlesham Hall (Fig. 11).

To protect new shoots and blossom on wall-trained fruit from frost, glass or canvas would often be used to form a removable screen that was placed

Fig. 11: Brick arch in the foundations of a disused melon pit at Hintlesham Hall. © J. A. Broster

Fig. 12: Glass screen against a wall to promote ripening of fruit. Taken from Beeton's New Book of Garden Management, *1871. Courtesy of Susan Campbell*

Fig. 13: Wall bracket for protective screen at Hintlesham Hall. © Tina Ranft

in front of the walls (Fig. 12). Glass appears to have been used at Sudbourne Hall, although only the supporting iron bolts – evenly spaced at 6 inch (15.24 centimetres) centres – still remain and probably date from the 1880s. The protective screen must have been successful because according to the 1934 sale particulars 'The south face of the [north] wall … is believed to be one of the finest peach growing walls in England'. At Glemham House and Hintlesham Hall supporting brackets can still be seen (Fig. 13). In the case of Hintlesham, the wall has numerous nail holes below the bracket line indicative of support for trained fruit. Brackets were also used to support rigid covers to protect fruit from dampness and water-splash, and thus minimise scab.

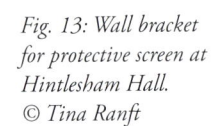

Glass, amongst other materials, could offer small and portable protection in the form of cloches, whilst clay pots were used to 'force' or blanch crops. Glass cloches varied in shape depending on their use. Lantern cloches were used to protect cuttings and crops, barn cloches for over-wintering crops, and the more fragile tent cloche had limited use but still offered some protection. The glass bell cloche had an inherent design fault, in that the knob on top could concentrate and strengthen the sun's rays and thus burn the crop inside. Remains of a considerable number of lantern cloches – as well as numerous frames and several glasshouses – have been found in the walled garden at Tendring Hall.

Lean-to and three-quarter span glasshouses were usually found on the south-facing side of a north wall. The wall would normally be painted with a whitewash – often lime

– to reflect the maximum sunlight and increase the amount of heat. Benhall Lodge is one of the many walled gardens in Suffolk to have remnants of whitewash on their walls that indicate where glasshouses once stood. Here, whitewash is visible continuously along the south side of the north wall, and also on the south side of the dividing wall. There is a recipe for soft putty that was used for colouring walls 'made with flour of whiting and cold, not boiled linseed oil' among historic gardener's notes for Broke Hall. Not all whitewash was made by this method. Lime plaster was used over knapped flints at The Old Rectory, Drinkstone, and may also have been used at Benhall. Lean-to glasshouses were often used as specialist houses rather than to grow a variety of plants. By 1839 Horringer Manor's walled garden had an internal glasshouse against its west wall, and later maps record that it had lengthened to 60 feet (18.29 metres). A lean-to glasshouse outside the garden at Horringer remains, and was manufactured locally by S. Smith & Company of Bury St Edmunds to a patent by Beard.

The design of free-standing glasshouses benefitted from technological advances and it is not easy to date the remains, or to differentiate between a frame and free-standing glasshouse when relying on map evidence. At Redisham Hall one of the glasshouses has been rebuilt, leaving only a stoke-hole and some of the piping from the original heating system, with a further complex of later free-standing glasshouses designed to match a series of older frames (Fig. 14). In Chantry Park's walled garden a large,

Fig. 14: The rebuilt glasshouse at Redisham Hall. Note the chimney at the end of the range. © J. A. Broster

modern free-standing glasshouse has been constructed on the site of an earlier, smaller glasshouse.

The importance of grapes as a dessert fruit led to the creation of specialist glasshouses from the late eighteenth century. In separate glasshouses water, ventilation and heat could be tailored to the grapes' exact needs, and thus ensure a healthy, long-lasting crop. The Victorian and Edwardian gardener was expected to supply his employer with hothouse grapes all the year round, and on large estates there were often two or three vineries.

The vine was not the only plant to have its own dedicated glasshouse. Depending on the owner's interests and wealth, other fruits such as peaches and nectarines were grown in separate houses within the walled garden, as were flowers such as carnations and orchids. A long range of glasshouses at Sudbourne Hall once included peach, fig and carnation houses. At Woodside large violets have been found recently that were previously grown in an adjacent sunken glasshouse. The 1920 sale catalogue for Rendlesham Hall refers to 'a range of 300 feet [91.44 metres] in length, consisting of a fig house, two peach houses and a nectarine house'. Both Rendlesham Hall and Sudbourne Hall once had further glasshouses to house vines.

BUILDINGS

The technological and production advances of the nineteenth century brought about the need for a wider range of buildings related to the work of the walled garden. While fruit and vegetable stores have been used for centuries, the need for a boiler house would only have occurred after the invention of cast-iron pipes and sophisticated boilers. Likewise, the standard of housing provided for the head gardener grew with his status, and the size of the bothy that housed the under-gardeners is an indication of the amount of labour required to tend the garden.

Today, many buildings related to walled gardens have been abandoned, become ruined or their use has changed. There are occasional remaining clues, such as a manger left in a corner of a former stable or the outline of a soot box in a former boiler room. Usually only fruit or vegetable stores are readily identifiable, and then only due to the remains of shelving or specialist tools. Glemham Hall has a surviving building that houses round-edged shelves that would once have been a fruit store, and at Horringer Manor the potting shed complex, although no longer in use, recently contained numerous interesting artefacts: puffers, the burners for Richard's Fumigators, bee-keeping equipment, an old seed drill marker and many earthenware pots.

Fortunately, there is still evidence of entire service ranges connected to walled gardens. These were also known as back sheds or back ranges. When constructed inside the garden they were invariably built against the coldest, north-facing wall, or they could be attached to the exterior of one of the

Fig. 15: Remains of a two-storey building at Tendring, which is thought to have been a bothy built over a mushroom house or potato store.
© J. A. Broster

walls – wherever they would not take up valuable growing space. Good examples survive at Bawdsey Manor, Glemham House and Rendlesham Hall. At Glemham House walled garden the range is attached to the outside, polygonal, north wall and once housed bothies – two of which remain, complete with fireplaces – a boiler house and what appears to have been a fruit store. Rendlesham Hall's service range was built on the north side of a dividing wall that carried south-facing glasshouses on the opposite side. The buildings once housed a single-storey vegetable store, a two-storey apple and pear store – the ground floor of which was later used as a potting shed – and two stalls that would have housed ponies or donkeys that worked in the garden. At the east end of the wall was a two-storey building (Fig. 15).

However, not all sites have the service range in the conventional position. Sudbourne Hall had a number of service buildings outside the garden. There were two free-standing ranges that stood beyond the south wall on either side of an entrance. These face north and backed onto south-facing glasshouses. They comprised open sheds, a mess room, two potting sheds, a heated mushroom house and a furnace or boiler room. Additionally, there was a bothy yard adjacent to the west wall. In this area, in 2008, there were the remains of a free-standing range of brick and reed-thatched buildings, including two thatched fruit stores, a vegetable store, pot store, office, open cart shed and potting shed. Opposite these, and backing onto the west wall

Fig. 16: The central range of service buildings at Benhall in 1987.
Courtesy Marion and Jim Mountain of The Walled Garden, Benhall

of the garden, were traces of coal and coke sheds, a men's earth closet and a brick and slate bothy.

The walled gardens of Benhall Lodge, Nowton Park and Thornham Hall have a central range of service buildings that divide the gardens approximately into two equal parts. In each, the service sheds are conventionally located on the north side of the dividing wall and behind west to east central greenhouse complexes. Figure 16 shows the central range at Benhall in 1987 – just before the hurricane of that year and later restoration. It comprised stores, potting shed and mushroom house. They have since been adapted for use as offices, stores and a plant sales area. At Nowton Park the service range consists of a bothy, machine shed, hay and straw store, stables, cart shed, boiler room, an open shed, potting shed, tool store and mushroom house. Inside the buildings there are the remains of their former use including a manger and boiler chimney, although since renovation has taken place – probably after the property came into the ownership of St Edmundsbury Borough Council – most of the building has been converted for use as general storage. Sometimes, service buildings are free-standing and adjacent to the walled garden. These are often fruit stores, like the one at Theberton House which stands outside the north-west corner of the garden and is surrounded by trees (Fig. 17). Sudbourne has a free-standing game larder near to the south wall. Figure 18 shows the interior of one of two fruit stores at Woodside. It is in a shaded area and is free-standing.

The boiler house, or engine room as it is sometimes known, provided power for heating in the garden. Usually, there was at least one in the back range, as at Glemham House. At Benhall at least three of the five boilers that were within the garden once heated the south-facing side of the north wall, serving heating systems with heavy 4 inch (100 centimetre) cast-iron pipes. The boiler house and storeroom were on the north side of the north wall. There was also an ancillary boiler house in the dividing range – its chimney is still visible today. This boiler would have been used to heat a vinery on the south-facing side (Fig. 19). Nowton Park also had a boiler in its dividing range, but there appears to be no surviving record of a boiler elsewhere in the garden. Glemham House had an additional boiler to that in its back sheds. This serviced a conservatory on the south side of the north wall. One of the many glasshouses at Redisham Hall had a boiler house at its northern end along with an accompanying coke hole, while Langham Hall has an interesting arrangement of a boiler complex for heating the wall and glasshouse that operated from the gardener's cottage

Fig. 17: The thatched fruit store at Theberton House. © Tina Ranft

Fig. 18: Inside one of two fruit stores at Woodside. © J. A. Broster

FEATURES: BUILDINGS

Fig. 19: The dividing range at Benhall from the south side, showing the chimney that is still visible today. This boiler would have been used to heat a vinery on this side. © Tina Ranft

Fig. 20: Langham Hall gardener's cottage, incorporated into the wall. © J. A. Broster

(Fig. 20). For safety reasons many boilers have been removed from their buildings, although some remain such as at Abbots Hall and Woodside.

From the early Victorian period until the 1900s, head gardeners enjoyed an impressive status and much prestige, and this was reflected in the size and quality of their accommodation. The head gardener's cottage was always close to the garden, and often had its own entrance into the garden. At Benhall the gardener lived in a thatched cottage to the north of the garden, photographed and still standing in the first half of the twentieth century (Fig. 21). By 2006 the cottage had completely collapsed and only a pile of rubble remained. The head gardener's house at Glemham House stands outside the south-east corner of the garden, east of the stables and close to the house. Some gardener's cottages were attached to the actual walls of the garden. Examples include Langham Hall, where the cottage was built by 1832 (see Fig. 20). Also attached to the walled garden is the gardener's cottage at Nowton. It is in the cottage orné style and appears to date from *c.* 1877, reflecting the high status of the head gardener at that time, who had previously worked at Sandringham and was said to be 'an eminent pomologist' (Fig. 22). At Chantry Park the cottage is on the north side of the north wall. Its back wall was originally the rear wall of the south-facing glasshouse behind it. A two-storey bothy and various stores are attached to the west side of the cottage.

Whilst the gardener's house or cottage provided the domestic dwelling for the head gardener, the bothy provided living quarters for his junior and under-gardeners. The bothy was often part of the service range, as at

Fig. 21: The gardener's cottage at Benhall in the first half of the twentieth century. Courtesy Marion and Jim Mountain of The Walled Garden, Benhall

Fig. 22: Nowton Park cottage orné style head gardener's cottage, dating from c. 1877.
© J. A. Broster

Chantry Park, Glemham House, Rendlesham Hall and Sudbourne Hall. The size of an estate would be reflected by the size and number of bothies. Five gardeners per acre (0.40 hectares) was the norm. The walled garden at Sudbourne Hall, at *c.* 2 acres (0.40 hectares), could be expected to have had ten gardeners. With two sharing a room, five bedrooms would have been required. The bothy at Sudbourne had six bedrooms – an indication that the garden was adequately staffed. At Saxham Hall the bothy was described in 1924 as having a sitting room, four cubicles, kitchen, scullery, electric light with hot and cold water laid on, which would have been extremely luxurious for bothy accommodation. The 1922 sale catalogue mentions that the bothy at Rendlesham Hall 'would make a nice house for an under-gardener, having three bedrooms, sitting room, kitchen and pantry'.

During the twentieth century many estates were broken up and sold. As a result, a number of walled gardens are now in separate ownership from the house and estate.

CASE STUDIES

ABBOT'S HALL, STOWMARKET

The rear of Abbot's Hall looking over the area that was once the pleasure gardens, with the walled garden to its right. © Edward Martin

Never had the crunch of a spade on a lower level of gravel been so exciting – or so it seemed at the time of Suffolk Gardens Trust's earliest venture in exploring walled gardens at Abbot's Hall in April 2005, which was also marked by our first timid attempts at garden archaeology. The walled garden at Abbot's Hall is part of a site covering *c.* 70 acres (28.31 hectares), comprising formal gardens, a canal, raised walk, and a fine Queen Anne style mansion. Since 1967 the site has been the home of the Museum of East Anglian Life (MEAL), at the bequest of the Longe family.[1]

The walled garden first appears on the Tithe Map of Stowmarket (1839). It is shown in greater detail in the sale catalogue of 1858 and on the 1885 OS map.[2] Lying east of the mansion, it is bordered to the north by an area of rough grassland and mature mixed planting – including beech and yew – once known as 'Camping Land'.[3] The slip garden to the east is planted with conifers – mainly yew – and probably dates from the first half of the last century. To the south is an area of grassland, and in 2005 there was a small modern glasshouse outside the garden towards its western end. Both the hall and garden were created by Charles Blosse, younger son of Thomas Blosse of Belstead Hall, a highly successful cloth merchant of Ipswich. Thomas Blosse rebuilt the hall *c.* 1709 and at the same time laid out the garden in the formal style of the period, with rectangular beds[4] that appear essentially unchanged in 1839. Later maps show that a conservatory[5] had been added to the east wall by 1885. By 1926 a lean-to glasshouse had been erected within the garden[6] and a potting shed had been built on the external side of the north wall.[7]

Map from sale catalogue, 1858. The walled garden is marked '297', attached to the right of the mansion. SRO (Ipswich) HE402/1/1858/19 Courtesy SRO

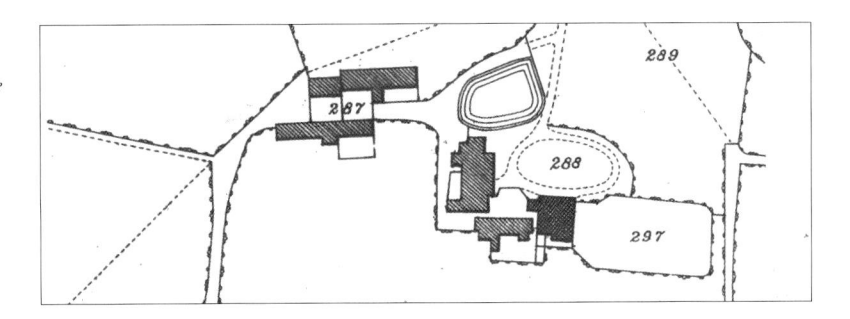

Apart from these maps and the sale catalogue of 1858, investigation into the early history of the garden was greatly hindered by the lack of documentary evidence. What had this garden been used for? Its appearance in 2005 was somewhat unprepossessing, following years of neglect. There was little to indicate what had originally been grown there. The western boundary was formed by a yew hedge, under-planted with box. There were no stumps of felled trees, a scattering of lupins and roses and a sweet bay, with two espaliered fig trees at the west and east ends of the north wall. Some of the brickwork is of the later eighteenth and more of the nineteenth centuries. The walls form an irregular rectangle, but the fact that in the north-east corner the shape of the garden is curved – describing a concave arc towards its western end – suggests this dates from the early nineteenth century when curved south-facing walls became popular for fruit growing. There were some fixing nails and straps on the inside of the east wall, but by far the majority were on the outer side of the southern wall, suggesting the importance of the slip garden for growing fruit, and strengthening our opinion that throughout its history this garden was mainly ornamental rather than productive.

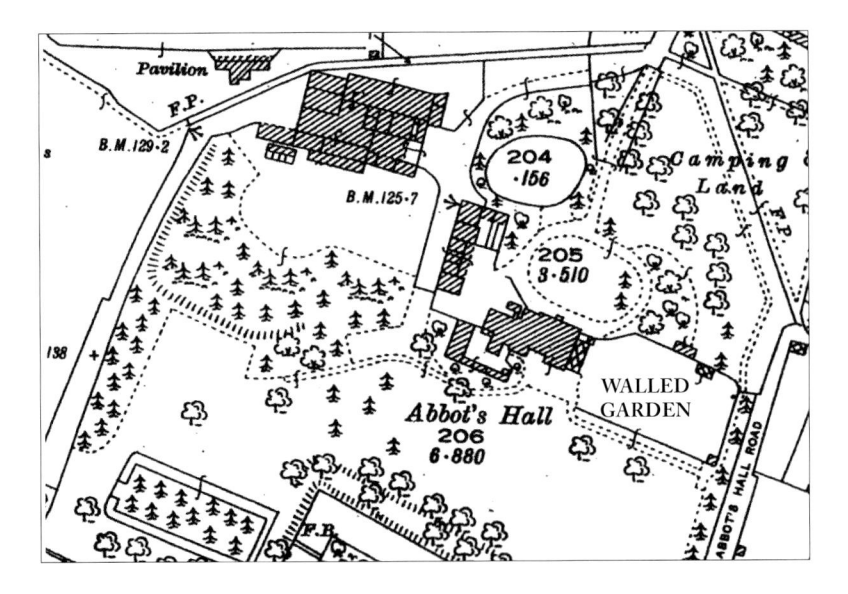

OS 3rd edition map, 1926. Courtesy of Ordnance Survey

28 WALLED GARDENS OF SUFFOLK

Two additional developments reinforced this view. Metal detection in the garden, carried out by the musician Bill Wyman in 2005, uncovered a number of rose labels, but dating only from the late nineteenth and early twentieth centuries. The earliest three hybrid perpetual roses – 'Dupuy Jamin' (1868), 'Alfred K. Williams' (1877) and 'Ulrich Brunner' (1882) – could belong to the period of garden layout shown on the 1885 OS map, while the later labels range from 1891 to 1953.

In March of the same year, Sally Kington, the International Daffodil Registrar of the Royal Horticultural Society Survey, carried out an investigation on the daffodils at Abbot's Hall. Her preliminary opinion was that, with the exception of a group of twentieth-century varieties at the north-west end of the original formal lawn south of the house, the majority of the daffodils seem to predate those that were named and classified at a major Royal Horticultural Society conference in 1885. They appear to be trumpet varieties of perhaps the 1870s, with doubles of seventeenth to eighteenth century date in the walled garden itself, such as 'Telamonius Plenus', 'Thomas Virescent Daffodil' and 'Orange Phoenix' (syn. 'Eggs and Bacon').[8]

In 2009, the museum began a programme to restore the walled garden in collaboration with Suffolk Mental Health Partnership NHS Trust, as part of a £6,000 project to aid recovery. 'Living Valued Lives' patients

South side of north wall of the garden showing the lean-to glasshouse and gate leading to the potting shed on the other side of the wall.
© *Tina Ranft*

The potting shed on the other side of the north wall.
© *Tina Ranft*

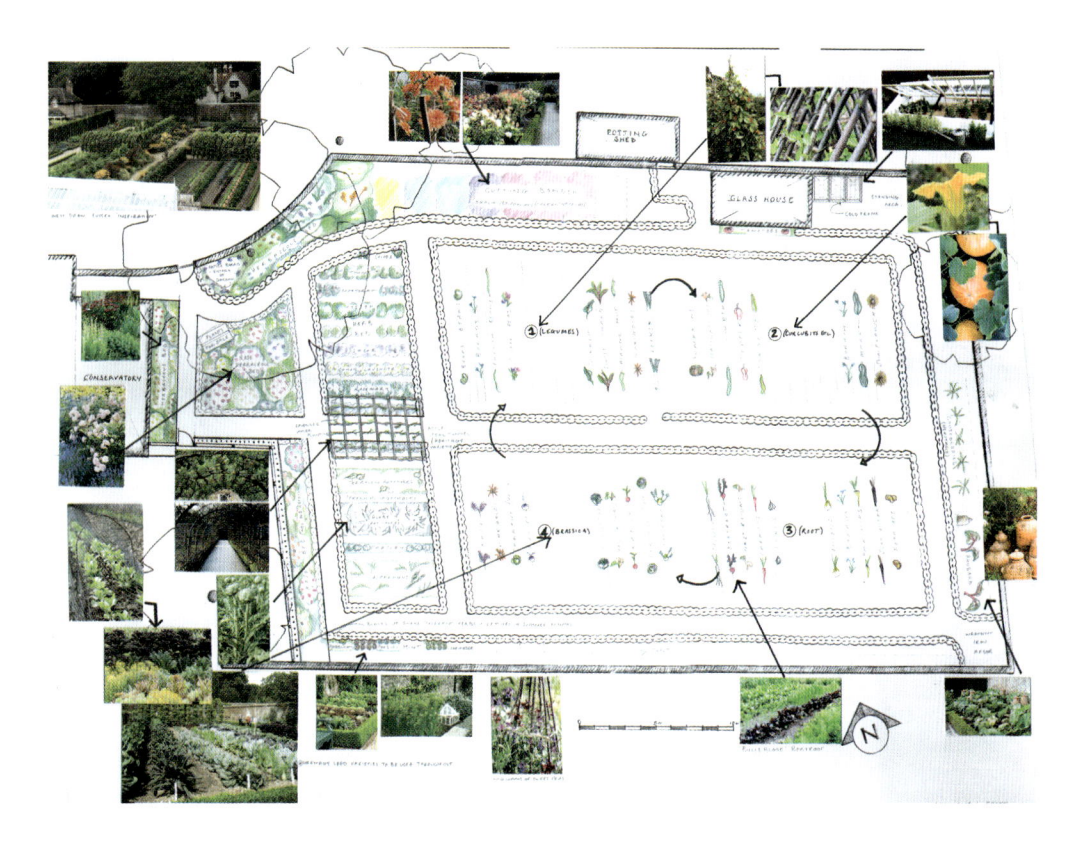

Modern planting plan by Lucy Spofforth, used as the basis for the restoration programme. Courtesy Lucy Spofforth

helped to maintain the garden while learning horticultural skills in the process, in a socially inclusive environment. In the course of this two-year programme some twenty of them dug, weeded and planted their way to mental well-being – clearing overgrown areas of the garden, planting borders with flowers and also making a herb garden, while growing a range of vegetables and rejuvenating the walled garden in the process.[9]

The museum continues to promote mental health service users, working alongside other volunteers to make up the workforce in the garden. Since 2013 it has been run as a Victorian kitchen garden with productive areas of vegetables, trained fruit trees, herb bed and cutting border. The two largest rectangular beds are the main vegetable growing areas. New box hedging has been planted to redefine the layout of the paths as shown on the OS map of 1885. There are plans to plant more heritage varieties of fruit trees – all East Anglian cultivars. The organically grown fruit and vegetables supply the museum café and are sold twice weekly on a stall close by, which helps to pay for seeds and equipment for the walled garden.

BARTON MERE HOUSE, GREAT BARTON

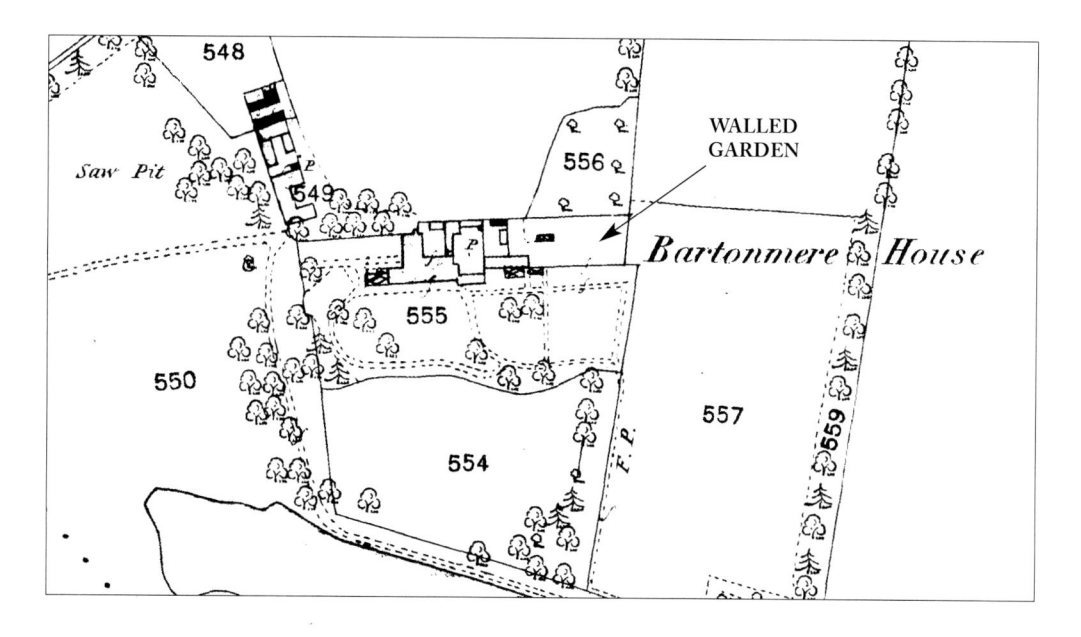

OS 1st edition map, 1884. Courtesy of Ordnance Survey

Barton Mere takes its name from the lake that forms the boundary between the parishes of Pakenham and Great Barton. The lake varies seasonally and depending on rainfall – at its largest it can be 10 acres (4.05 hectares) in size. It borders the formal gardens and is clearly visible from the gate leading into the walled garden, which meant there was a constant supply of water, and so there was no need for a dipping pool and numerous pumps. A remaining ancient pump provides evidence of how water was delivered to the garden. The unique feature of this garden is that it defies the generalisations that can be made about the siting and size of walled gardens, in that it is a linear garden aligned to the Georgian façade of a much earlier house, with the ornamental gardens accessed from it and providing a slip garden. In addition, it is also unusual because it is accessed from two courtyards at the rear of the house, which formerly contained a dairy and fruit store and other services, including a brewery and an underground boiler house that heated the glasshouses. These lead into a further service area, with more pumps, and with access into the productive walled garden.

Barton Mere House appears on Hodskinson's 1783 *Map of Suffolk*,[1] but it is recorded earlier that 'it is an old mansion constructed of brick ... which formerly belonged to the L'Estrange family and in 1728 it passed by marriage to Captain Curwen, from whom the late Reverend Henry Jones inherited it'. By the time of the 1843 Tithe Award for Pakenham it was recorded that the park and garden amounted to some 3 acres (1.2 hectares), the walled garden and house are about 1 acre (0.40 hectares).[2] At that time it was occupied by Thomas Quayle Esq. Later intermarriage between the

Barton Mere House in 1957, showing the three-quater span glasshouse attached to the west elevation. SRO (Bury) K 513. Courtesy SRO

Quayle and Jones family meant that it remained in continuous ownership until the early 20th century. In 1961 it was purchased by Charles Murton Webb, father of the present owner.

Captain Curwen was responsible for alterations to the property that remained unchanged until the present owners undertook further restoration. Today's owners hold a document entitled 'The Plan of the Garden to the South of Captain Curwen's House in Barton, in Suffolk, taken by Wm. Warren, 1738'. Warren was a member of a Bury St Edmunds based firm of surveyors, active in the early part of the nineteenth century. The plan shows the gardens to be very typical of their time with flowerbeds and fishponds – most of which have since gone. A tinted drawing of the house is shown on the plan and it has been inferred that it was Curwen who was responsible for the Georgian façade, as well as the substantial stable block and agricultural buildings to the north-west of the house. The present owners said that this complex housed cows, hence the dairy.

The OS map of 1884 shows a glasshouse appended to the west end of the house. Photographs dating from 1975 in Suffolk Record Office[3] show a three-quarter span glasshouse that would be consistent with that shown on the map. This type of glasshouse was usually used as a vine house, with the vines planted outside and threaded into the glasshouse. The older glasshouse has now been replaced with a modern conservatory on the same footprint.

At the east end of the house there was a further glasshouse, now replaced by a modern Alitex glasshouse, though still containing an older pump. Adjacent to this glasshouse there had been another glasshouse facing out into the pleasure garden. This, however, no longer exists. Nearby, there is a gate into the walled garden. Though now restored, there is still ample

The north and east walls of the garden, showing the random nature of the materials and construction used.
© *Tina Ranft*

evidence of the activities of the brick and flint walled service area, including a pantiled potting shed and further stores.

The walls of the kitchen garden are an interesting mixture of brick and flint together with conventional brickwork for the south wall. This is flat-faced on the pleasure garden side with no plinth or buttresses – these being found on the inside facing wall – and provide the strength for this tall wall of 8 feet rising to 12 feet (2.43 to 3.65 metres). The wall is liberally peppered with nail holes used for supporting fruit and some old trees remain, plus numerous old rectangular zinc labels – mostly illegible – one of which says 'Conference 1930'.

Returning inside the walled garden, the north and east walls are unique. Whether it was for economy or due to eccentricity, they are made up of flints, brick, slate, over-burnt bricks (overburns) and even bottles. There are some portions that are built in conventional courses, but for the major part there is no discernible pattern or design, just material laid in lime mortar. Despite what has been said in the past about the lesser longevity and stability of flint walls, this wall has remained in a good state of repair, or perhaps it is that the random nature of the construction means that repair would not be as obvious as in a conventional brick wall.

In what is a very personal and charming garden, integrated closely with the house, one final unique feature remains to be commented on. East of the east wall of the walled garden, which extends south to enclose the pleasure garden, is a very old multi-stemmed vine. The owners say that it has cropped variably, producing small very sour grapes. When the annual growth reached the top of the wall, it was trained over onto the west-facing aspect of the wall so that the fruit could benefit from the afternoon sun. This could, perhaps, be described as the most extreme example of 'slip' culture!

LANGHAM HALL, LANGHAM

Aerial photograph of the walled garden taken in the 1960s. The temple backed up by a potting shed is shown far left with the other building in the foreground being the gardener's cottage.
Courtesy Phil Mizen of Langham Herbs

The first thing that the visitor sees on entering the walled kitchen garden at the north end of the west wall is a complex of buildings, most of which have been restored and are currently in use as offices. Both single and two-storey, these are presumably former service buildings of the garden. Evidence of what appears to be a series of nine bricked-up windows is a further sign of its continuing evolving use from the early eighteenth century onwards[1] when Henry and John Turnor's Account Book reveals a purchase of mulberries and lemons in 1705, and a year later a payment of '6 shillings' to 'Sargeant the gardener' for trees.[2]

The present hall dates from the 1740s and was built by Sir Peter Blake, MP for Sudbury, whose wealth was derived from sugar plantations on the West India islands of St Kitts and Montserrat, who had purchased it from the Turnor family of Bury St Edmunds, owners since 1672.[3] Sir Peter was largely responsible for the layout of the garden and the neighbouring pleasure grounds as they are today.[4] In the sale to the Maitland Wilsons in 1832 the kitchen garden is described as '4 acres of garden ground, walled with lofty brick walls, in 4 divisions, with choice fruit trees in full bearing, and a neat gardener's cottage, conservatory, hot-houses, grapery, and hot walls for the forcing of fruit'.[5] An inventory of the kitchen garden's contents, taken in the same year, lists:

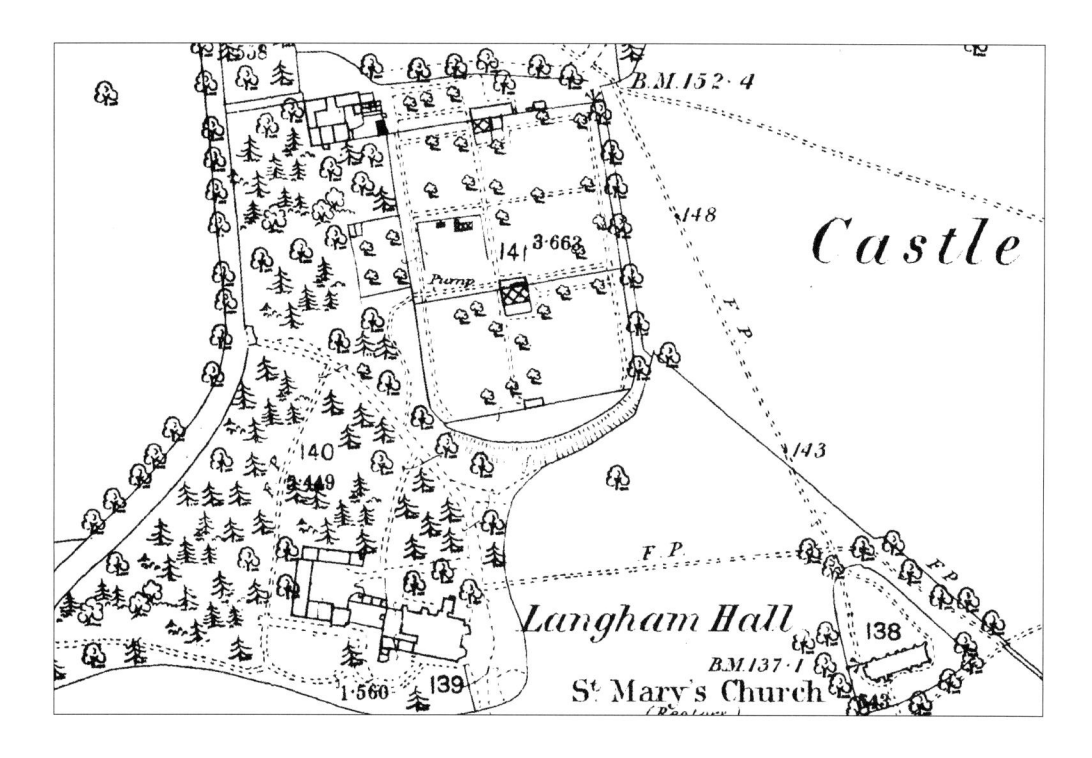

OS 1st edition map, 1884. Courtesy of Ordnance Survey

'Iron roll[er] – one cucumber double frame-single ditto and light-sundry sea kale pots etc – sundry tools. 2 wheelbarrows – 2 ladders, 2 watering cans, shelves in chambers, Sundry old light frames – long ladders – 4 stoves in gardener's house. Truck cart – flower stages – flower barrow – water tub – 12 linen posts, sun dial on stone pillar.'[6]

During the Victorian period the hall was frequently let or unoccupied – close by Stowlangtoft Hall having become the family's main residence, which was rebuilt by the wealthy Henry Wilson in 1859, and where the future Edward VII was a frequent guest from the 1880s onwards. It seems likely that produce from the kitchen garden at Langham not only helped to provide for the family and its visitors, but also supplied its residence in nearby Bury St Edmunds. A garden of more than 3.5 acres (*c.* 1.50 hectares) in extent would have no problem whatsoever in achieving this.

The kitchen garden shown on the Ordnance Survey map of 1884[7] abuts onto the pleasure grounds, a few hundred yards to the north-east of the hall. It is rectangular in shape, its four quarters marked with grass paths, and with a central dividing path that is clearly visible today. Built onto the north wall, the original gardener's cottage survives, its south wall contiguous with that of the garden wall itself, and unusually contains the boiler house that originally heated the wall and the lost glasshouse – perhaps the hot wall and vinery mentioned in the 1832 inventory. Two of the cold frames remain, and in addition there is a small modern glasshouse dating from the

Front view of temple (top) which is backed-up by a potting shed (right). Courtesy Margaret Bampton

1980s. The windows of the cottage give a clear view of most of the kitchen garden, including the storeroom or potting shed – with accommodation above – which is built against its southern wall. In the upper eastern quarter of the garden there are several fruit trees – some at least 50 years old – with a number of even older examples dating from the 1920s and 1930s along the garden's north–south axis. The remaining walls, both outside and inside the garden, reveal nail holes and examples of straining wires – all signs of former extensive fruit cultivation.

That the garden was highly productive is beyond doubt, in that the provision of water was impressive and unusual. A traditional dipping pond is not a feature, but there is a well-constructed and very deep well in the south-west corner with a pump that is shown on the Ordnance Survey map of 1884. In the complex of service buildings in the north-west corner there is a covered cistern used to collect run-off water from all the roofs.

However, by far the most interesting feature – apart from the impressive range of brick walls – is the inner three-sided walled area occupying much of the garden's south-western quarter. This is a garden within a garden,

View of the garden showing a walled area within the outer walls.
© *Tina Ranft*

facing south, that ensures additional shelter and warmth. It may have been fully enclosed by the nineteenth century, though only the northern and eastern walls appear on the 1904 Ordnance Survey map.[8] Since then the western wall has been replaced, leaving the southern side open. Eight espalier fruit trees now line the inner side, with twelve on the outer, forming an unusual example of slip cultivation, but yielding no clues as to what it may have originally contained.

Langham is unusual in that beyond the south wall of the productive garden the walls continue to form a pleasure garden with an impressive gateway and wrought iron gates that lead directly to Langham Hall. In the centre of the boundary wall, between productive and pleasure gardens, there is a building unique in our experience – on the productive side it is a potting shed in the rustic style, with pantiled roof, and on the pleasure ground side it is a delightful pavilion complete with Doric columns.

Today the kitchen garden continues to be a fully working unit, specialising in herbs and fruit, and in addition it holds the National Collection of Alpine Campanulas.[9] A photograph taken in the 1960s shows the garden to have been highly productive. Perhaps Langham's survival owes much to the fact that Stowlangtoft became the Maitland Wilsons' main residence, thus sparing the massive improvements and extensions that might otherwise have resulted.[10] That it benefited from this comparative neglect is certain, while it was equally fortunate in avoiding military occupation during World War II, which hastened the destruction of much grander Suffolk houses such as Sudbourne Hall, and the loss of their kitchen gardens.

NOWTON PARK (formerly Nowton Court), BURY ST EDMUNDS

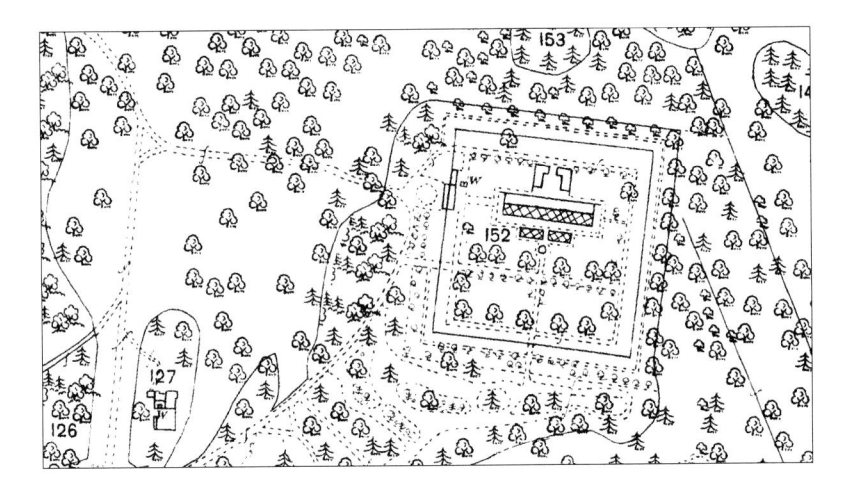

OS 1st edition map 1884. Courtesy of Ordnance Survey

Nowton Park's walled garden stands out from many of the others recorded by Suffolk Gardens Trust in that surviving records provide useful insights into the financial aspects of such projects – in this case, set against the property's history from the time it was bought by Orbell Oakes, son of the banker James Oakes, in 1802 until its eventual purchase by St Edmundsbury Borough Council in 1985. Nowton Park is the only Suffolk walled garden surveyed where plans and estimates are extant and where the subsequent changes in execution can be traced.

From 1817 onwards Orbell Oakes – who enjoyed gardening, shooting and fishing – extended what was little more than a cottage orné, spending nearly £2,500 on land and buildings to develop what was described as 'an elegant mansion in the Tudor-style, surrounded by a beautiful park and garden' – as good a summary of his achievement as any.[1] A plan of the Nowton estate made in 1832 shows 'Gardens and Plantations' extending to some 3 acres (1.21 hectares), roughly quadrilateral in shape, close to the house, divided into four sections by a series of paths, with a building – possibly a conservatory – in the north west corner.[2]

But it was not until 1875, when J. H. F. Oakes inherited the estate, that there were further substantial changes, with the extension of the park to *c.* 200 acres (494.19 hectares) and the construction of a walled garden, about a quarter of a mile distant from the house. This occurred between 1876 and 1878 and was based on a series of plans and drawings by the London architect Henry J. Bacon. These plans, together with estimates and correspondence between Oakes, Bacon and various manufacturers and builders, give a clear picture of Oakes's thinking and how the scheme evolved.

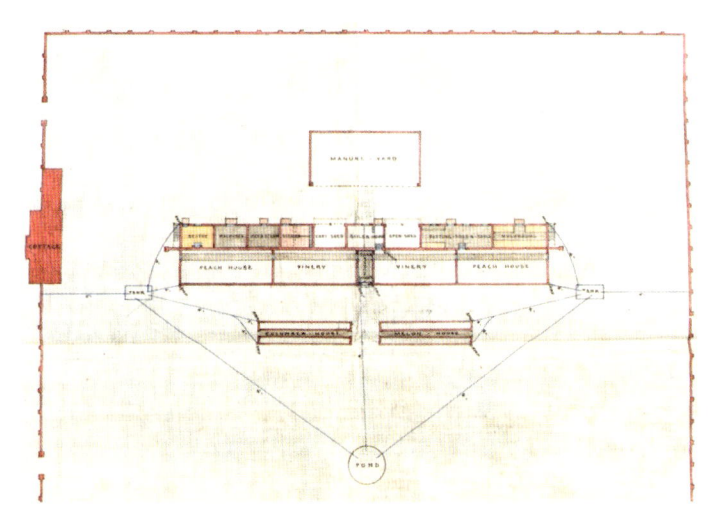

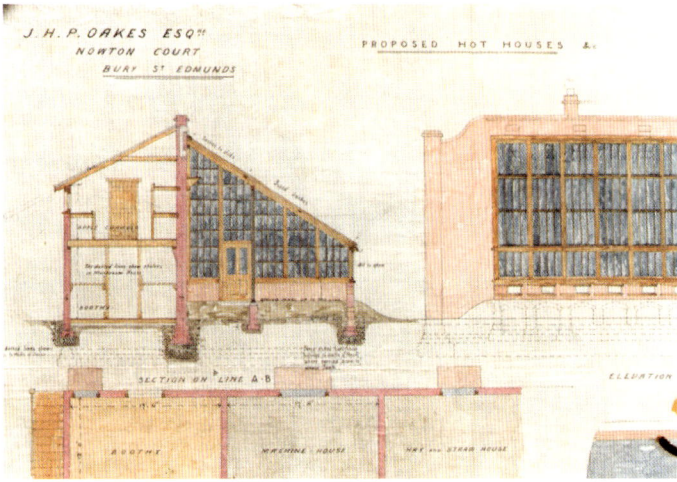

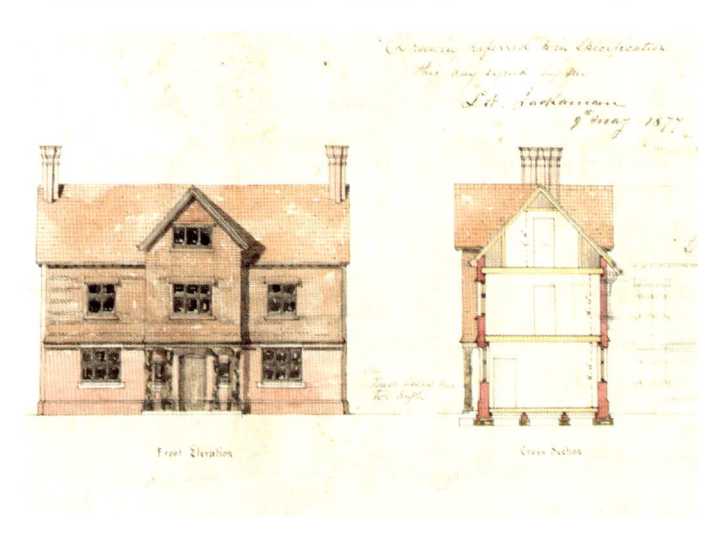

The 1876 to 1878 series of plans and drawings for the walled garden by London architect Henry J. Bacon. (Top) Showing the gardener's cottage to the left and central service range with bothies and sheds backing onto the peach and vinery houses. (Middle) Section of the hot houses and bothies behind, and to the right a partial elevation of the hot houses. (Bottom) Design for the gardener's cottage. Courtesy St Edmundsbury Council

James and Arthur Gray of Chelsea provided an estimate of £18,880 for the vinery, cucumber and melon houses on 1st April 1878. However, just over two months later on 7th June a lower figure of £1070 12s 0d was accepted from James Boyd & Son (Hot-House Builders) and Henry Eyres of Paisley near Glasgow, while the firm of J. J. Thomas & Co of Paddington secured the bid for the wall fittings – the brass and copper straining screws that are such an unusual feature of the garden's walls.[3] The only contractor with a local interest was Lot Jackman (builder and mason) of 1 Westgate Street in Bury St Edmunds. His successful bid for the building work amounted to £3,907 10s 0d, which included £773 10s 10d for the head gardener's cottage. Taking the other surviving estimates into consideration, it is likely that Oakes spent between £10,000 and £11,000 on the entire project – if Bacon the architect's fee is also included.[4]

Today the walled garden covers *c.* 2.960 acres (1197.9 hectares) and is surrounded by woodland, with main access through a wide gate in the west wall. It is unusual in that it has no wall-hung glasshouses, just one centrally placed free-standing building parallel to the garden's north wall, *c.* 54 yards (50 metres) in length orientated east–west, and equidistant from its eastern and western walls. This is clearly shown on the OS map of 1885.[5] Between the glasshouses and the south wall the garden is laid out in a traditional fashion – divided into quarters with a dipping pond placed slightly north of the intersecting paths that no longer remain. Erected in 1989, six ranges of modern horticultural glasshouses cover a section of the east quarter. Further glasshouses, or possibly frames, to the north of the originals and shown on the 1904 OS map, have since disappeared.

Comparing Bacon's extensive plans and drawings with what remains today suggests that the walls of the free-standing glasshouses and service buildings were not built according to the architect's original specification, which required that 'jumps should be included to account for level changes'. As Lot Jackman was responsible for the original clearing and ground work, it is probable that he levelled the ground to abate the need for such changes, or achieved them through the downward curve at the junction of the south wall with those of the east and west end. A more significant deviation from Bacon's original plan is revealed in the same free-standing glasshouse and service complex. Though now demolished, the footings of the glasshouses were constructed according to the plans, but the service buildings backing on to them are radically different. All the plans indicate that they could have been substantially narrower and the front wall higher. This provided an upper storey accessed by external stairs for bothy accommodation and an apple store. According to further plans, it also appears that the south elevation was a glasshouse and the north provided open and closed storage. However, the doors and openings corresponded to the Bacon design, i.e. from right (the west end) they were in sequence: a bothy, machine shed, hay and straw store, stables, a cart

North side of the central service range today.
© J. A. Broster

shed, boiler room, an open shed, potting and machine sheds and a mushroom house. One of the sheds was lined with tongue and groove timber and probably served as an office. The glasshouses included peach houses and two vineries.[6]

The head gardener's cottage is an imposing structure built into the west wall. It is a three-storey building with a single-storey extension to the north and has five bedrooms, which includes two attic rooms. The style is cottage orné with a touch of Arts and Crafts – the front elevation being tile hung at first and second-storey level, the porch incorporating four tree trunks used as pillars with an entablature that is painted to represent stone. The appearance and size of the house reflects the status of Mr Carmichael the head gardener at Nowton from 1876 to 1883, who had previously worked at Sandringham. Under his charge, in addition to espaliered varieties of pear that included Jargonelle, Mariette de Millepieds and Doyenne Robin, apple trees were planted in three rows on two sides outside the walls – a good example of slip culture – while inside single rows of broccoli or sprouts were grown between rows of asparagus, together with large beds of strawberries, and the extensive glasshouses contained melons, pears, grapes and cucumbers.[7]

St Edmundsbury Borough Council purchased the Nowton estate in 1985 and work soon began on transforming the old walled garden into the new base for the borough nurseries. Today it is being used productively to rear plants with a vegetable box scheme centred on the garden. It is also used as a therapeutic horticultural centre for students with learning disabilities. There are plans to use the park and garden as a wedding venue and to refurbish the head gardener's cottage for use as a holiday let.

RENDLESHAM HALL (formerly Rendlesham White House), RENDLESHAM

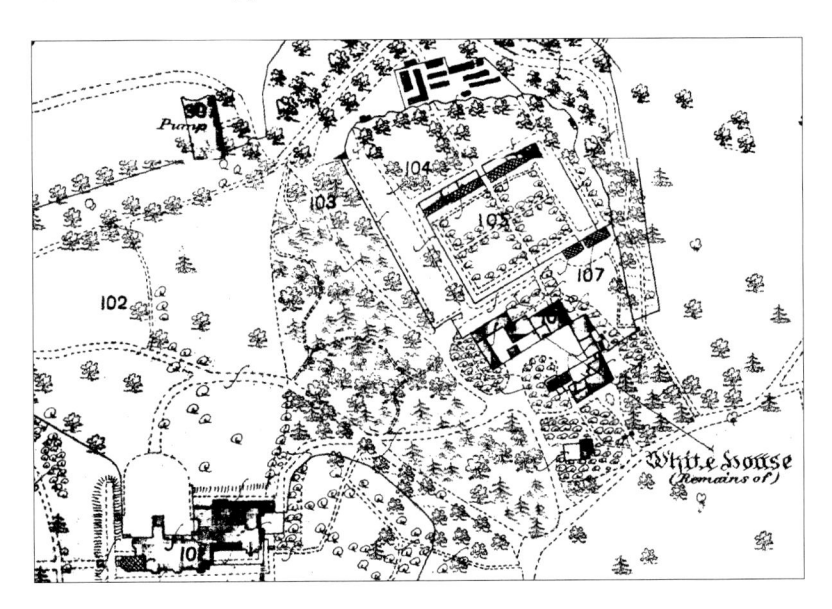

OS 1st edition map 1881/2. Courtesy of Ordnance Survey

Rendlesham Park – clearly shown on John Hodskinson's *Map of Suffolk* (1783) – is situated some five miles from Woodbridge and three to the south-east of Wickham Market in an area now largely owned by the Forestry Commission. It was purchased by the wealthy London banker Peter Thelusson, later the first Lord Rendlesham, from Lord Archibald Hamilton in 1796.[1]

The hall (formerly known as Rendlesham White House) was enlarged and altered in the gothic style by Henry Hakewill in 1801 to the design of J. B. Papworth. The surrounding park was laid out to designs by Humphrey Repton. A second mansion – built following a fire in 1830 and described as 'a large and handsome mansion of flint and stone, delightfully situated in a extensive park' – is shown on the Tithe Map of 1840, though on too small a scale to show the walled garden.[2] Thus it is not until the 1880s, with the publication of the Ordnance Survey map of 1887[3] and an article in *The Gardener's Chronicle* for 1881,[3] that a clear picture emerges of an impressive garden of over 4 acres (1.62 hectares) situated close to the original White House – perhaps suggesting it is sixteenth- or seventeenth-century in origin. An 1840 map reveals a garden divided into four rectangular sections with a central path bounded on the north side by an extensive range of glasshouses and frames, with a further irregular shaped area of similar size bounded by a semi-circular wall. This is typical of a size and layout for walled gardens approved by John Claudius Loudon, and appropriate to the support of the wealthier gentry and nobility. Apart from the surviving crinkle-crankle wall that may date from the eighteenth century, the style of the remainder suggests that it was created in the 1850s and 1860s by either the 4th Lord Rendlesham (1798–1852) or his successor the 5th Baron Thelusson (1840–1901). It would have provided fruit and vegetables all the year round for family, friends and guests – which it did on a prodigious scale. Many gardens of its size and wealthy ownership would have had hot walls for peaches and nectarines and pits or glasshouses for melons and pineapples. By 1800 the cost to run such a garden would have amounted to *c*. £400 a year, which could include about £30 for seeds, tools, pots and the rest, £85 for the head gardener, and the remainder split between casual labour and coal for heating.[4]

The entrance into the garden in the south-west corner of the complex. © Tina Ranft

'T.B.', writing in *The Gardener's Chronicle*, praised the then head gardener, Mr Mills, for his energy in developing the garden over the previous twelve years, above all for the quality of produce in the kitchen garden:

> 'The principal fruit-houses ... are lean-to's, about 300 feet in length, divided into seven compartments, at one time warmed by flues, but now by hot water, and are a useful lot, well adapted for grapes and peaches, which are grown remarkably well, the grapes especially having the finish about them in colour and bloom that mark successful cultivation. Commencing at the western end, the first house is filled with a mixed lot composed of Black Hamburghs, Madresfield Court, Lady Downe's and Black Alicante, bearing a very good crop ... the next division are all late sorts – Black Alicante, Lady Downe's and Trebbiano ... these also are bringing on a good crop that promises well ... We then come to a house occupied by Muscats alone ... and they are now carrying a nice crop, evenly distributed from top to bottom of the house.'

Next followed peach houses, and two houses for forcing strawberries, before the writer arrived at the orchid house and thence to examine the hardy fruit culture. Among the espaliered pear trees were popular varieties such as Jargonelle, Winter Nelis and Louise Bonne de Jersey, 'a fair crop of peaches and nectarines on the walls, and some apricots and a large number

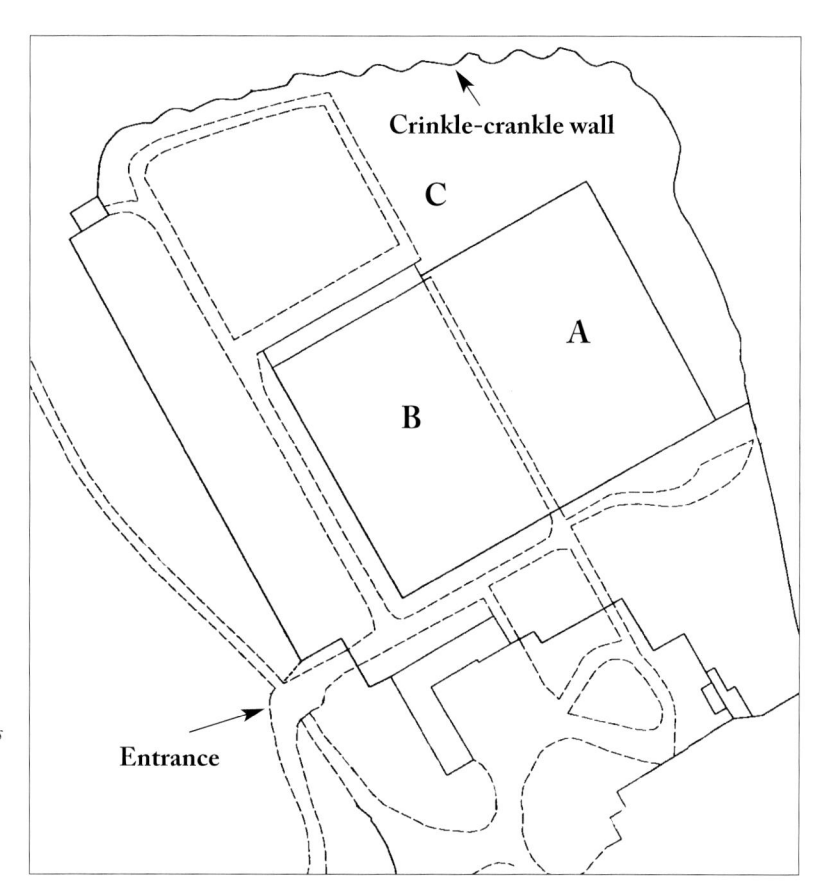

Main features of the garden including areas A, B, C, the crinkle-crankle wall and the main entrance, based on the OS 2005 map.

of pyramid pears and bush apples ... bearing a very fine crop', 'T.B.' considering that, 'Altogether there is much in the shape of good gardening to be seen at Rendlesham'.

A clear picture of the garden buildings emerges from the sale catalogues of 1920 and 1922:

> 'There is about 700 yards of massive brick walling, the majority being about 14 feet high and covered with choice fruit trees on the wall, some of the outside nectarine trees producing over 100 fruit in an average season. There is also over 650 feet of single span glasshouses comprising the following: Three malmaison houses, orchard house, two plant houses, two melon pits, fig house, two stove houses and cold frames, and in one of the inner gardens is a range about 300 feet in length, consisting of fig house, vinery, two peach houses, muscat house, one vinery and one greenhouse nectarine house. In the rose garden is a peach and nectarine house.'[5]

It was suggested that the bothy – consisting of three bedrooms, sitting room, kitchen and pantry – would make 'a nice house for an under

The south facing side of the dividing wall between areas B and C, showing where glasshouses once stood. © Tina Ranft

gardener'; nor does the 1920 catalogue fail to mention the potting shed, tool shed and mess room, fruit store room, packing shed and coal shed, all of which have survived in varying states of repair, along the central axis dividing areas **A** and **B** (see diagram opposite).[6] However, the same cannot be said of the remainder, for the range of glasshouses facing onto areas **A** and **B** of the map have long since disappeared, as have all but some traces of those on the west wall of area **B**. Nail holes in the walls and remnants of training wires are a sad reminder of espaliers long-vanished, although a few specimens – mostly apricot and cherry – survive on the east wall of area **B**. There are numerous cedars, limes and sweet chestnuts in the original shelter belt outside the earliest part of the walled garden bounded by a crinkle-crankle wall (area **C**). The few glasshouses outside the wall, dating from the 1920s, are in the final stages of dilapidation. Yet, at the time of a survey in 2005, the general condition of the walls was good and the garden was virtually empty, save for the remnants of a former Christmas tree nursery and some old espaliered pear trees.

Its history, following the sales of 1920 and 1922, parallels the fate of many such gardens. Despite the Agricultural Depression of the 1870s, the hall was rebuilt between 1868 and 1871, and for the last time after another disastrous fire in 1899. But a few years later, in 1903, it was let to the Norwich Sanitarium Company as a home for alcoholics and drug addicts, and purchased by the company in 1922 with 5,990 acres (2343.2 hectares) of the estate comprising the kitchen garden, park and other holdings. The kitchen garden may well have continued to be productive, as doctors

The crinkle-crankle wall bounding the earliest part of the garden as seen from area C.
© *Tina Ranft*

favoured gardening and other outdoor activities as part of their health programmes, and the fact that the large conservatory in the rose garden was rebuilt *c.* 1925 provides further evidence of continuity.[7]

In 1939 the hall was requisitioned for the war effort and was occupied at various times by the military and the Women's Land Army. It was finally demolished in 1949. The site, including the walled garden and a quantity of agricultural land, was bought by the family of the present owners in the early 1950s – a forebear having previously bought part of the Eyke Farm Estate, belonging to the original Rendlesham holdings in 1922.

There is an awesome quality about this garden. Stripped as it is of its former glories, the massive walls and proportions give it a grandeur and melancholy in keeping with its great house, swept away with the family whose prodigious wealth and ostentatious lifestyle it supported for well over a century. Perhaps Rendlesham is a Suffolk Heligan in waiting?

TENDRING HALL, STOKE-BY-NAYLAND

The curved north-west corner, which would have been the first glimpse of the walled garden from the hall.
© *Tina Ranft*

Tendring Hall, an outstanding example of the work of architect Sir John Soane, was commissioned by Sir Joshua Rowley Bt. in 1784, closely followed by an agreement with Humphry Repton, whose plans for the park included extending the existing pleasure grounds around the house and creating a range of walks. One such walk was to 'run under the lime trees to the stables and kitchen garden'.[1] The site of the walled garden, some 250 metres (273.5 yards) south-east of the house, is shown in the enclosure on a map of 1723, while the Tithe Map (1816) indicates that it was walled by that date.[2]

Both hall and grounds greatly benefited from their setting, which was unusually hilly for Suffolk and described in *The Gardener's Chronicle* for 1879:

> 'The manor stands on an eminence, a well wooded park commanding extensive views of the surrounding country, through which the Stour winds its gentle way … the lawn is a broad open expanse on a level with the park beyond with which it merges and forms a continuous sweep right on to the quiet village of Nayland, a mile and a half distant; while to the left a large portion of hill and dale in the county of Essex is open to view.'[3]

These heights are part of a ridge dividing the Stour valley in the north from the Box valley to the south, giving Tendring a picturesque river valley setting with the park falling away from the north ridge towards the valley floor

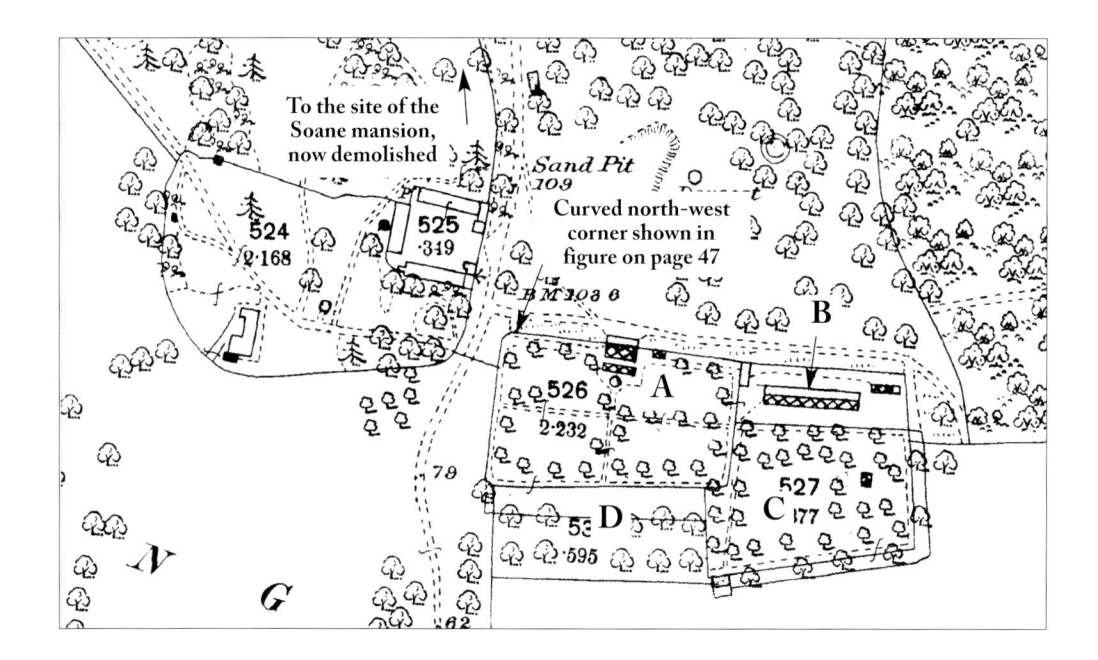

OS 2nd edition map 1886. Note the four separately walled areas marked A, B, C, D. Courtesy of Ordnance Survey

and the valley slopes to the south offering extensive views across the countryside.[4]

Tendring was let for much of the twentieth century and tenanted by David Davies in 1931, when the terms of the agreement included an obligation to maintain the gardens. However, a year later this was amended, allowing him to grass over the kitchen garden except for 1 acre (0.4047 hectares) that was to include the asparagus beds. Nothing was said regarding the lean-to vine and peach houses, which presumably were allowed to slide into gentle decline, drastically accelerated by the occupation of the hall by the army during World War II – from which it never recovered – and resulting in its demolition in 1954 with the eventual abandonment of the kitchen garden. At the time of a visit in 2010 the walled garden was given over to the rearing of pheasants and most of the remaining internal structures were in a ruinous condition.[5] The following description from the 1870s reveals a garden of considerable complexity, skillfully designed to meet the challenges of such a difficult site:

> '[it] lies well for forwarding early crops, the ground having a regular fall of 60 feet in 100 yards, and as the aspect is south, the winds are kept off from the opposite quarter, and the sun naturally beams great power on such sharp incline, the intersecting walls at different levels providing further shelter.'

These intersecting walls are clearly shown on the Ordnance Survey map of 1886, and they remain largely intact today. There is a curved outer wall around the main rectangular complex (A) with stone steps leading down

Above: From the north in area A (see OS map opposite), looking south towards the valley below, showing the sloping nature of the site and an impression of the huge size of each walled area. To the right are the remains of a dipping pond and cold frame brick base. © Tina Ranft

Below: The remains of a boiler cavity in area B. © J. A. Broster

to its various levels. The walls of red brick with white stone capping would have been visible from the house. This main kitchen garden of *c.* 4.61 acres (1.87 hectares) now comprises a single compartment with four subdivisions with a break in the walls to the west and east. Inside is a circular dipping well, and remains of the brick bases of glasshouses, frames and fragments of the boiler house. In the north-east compartment (B) there are curious remnants of a building, possibly a store, bothy, mushroom house or perhaps housing all three. Some remaining stone steps lead to the remnants of an orchard in area C of the garden complex and there are a few trees in area D, as shown on the Ordnance Survey map of 1886.[6]

The Gardener's Chronicle article of 1879 makes much of the hydraulic system devised to irrigate the kitchen garden, which was particularly needed because of

Remains of glasshouses on the south side of the north wall in area A (see OS map page 48). To the left is a lime washed wall with the remains of cold frames to the right. © Tina Ranft

the sandy soil and sloping site. Water pumped by a wheel from a well sunk into a stream was taken,

> 'to the top of the mansion, a height of 170 feet and from the tank there all the others will be kept filled and shut off by means of ball taps ... up to 400 gallons an hour.'[7]

Was Soane himself responsible for this complex water distribution system, and to what extent had he gained a knowledge of hydraulics from his early travels in Italy?[8] A closer look at some of his other projects might open up a wider study of the subject.[9]

THE WALLED GARDEN, HORRINGER MANOR (formerly Brooke House), HORRINGER

Centrally placed gates looking up from the lower garden. Note the trees in the background that were once part of the pleasure grounds. A surviving path leads through the trees towards the original manor house. (See OS map on page 52.)
© *Tina Ranft*

The Walled Garden, Horringer, is a splendid example of a kitchen garden closely integrated with the ornamental landscape of its park that is revealed on the Tithe Map (1839) showing Brooke House[1] and its surrounding pleasure grounds – possibly on the site of a malt house – one mile to the east of Horringer. This was at a time when most of the rest of the village belonged to the Earl of Bristol from nearby Ickworth.[2] All the available evidence suggests that the grounds were laid out by the owner Arthur Brooke, whose family owned the estate for much of the nineteenth century. More recently it has passed through the hands of several owners and the walled garden was sold into separate ownership *c*. 1998.[3]

Opposite the church and entrance to Ickworth Park is a lane leading from the A143. Horringer Manor is to be found on the left and The Walled Garden on the right. The garden is on a sloping site running down to a small stream on a north–west to south–east orientation. It consists of two gardens, the upper and smaller has a rounded wall at the north-west end, which is bounded by a yew hedge of some age to form a surviving walk, behind which is a wood of oak and yew planted alternatively, and a path that leads to a gate on the Horringer Manor side of the road. This confirms information supplied by a former employee that the walled garden featured as part of the pleasure ground walks and would account for many of its decorative features.

An ornate wrought iron gate leads into the upper garden through the yew hedge – one of a series of three aligned gates leading down to the

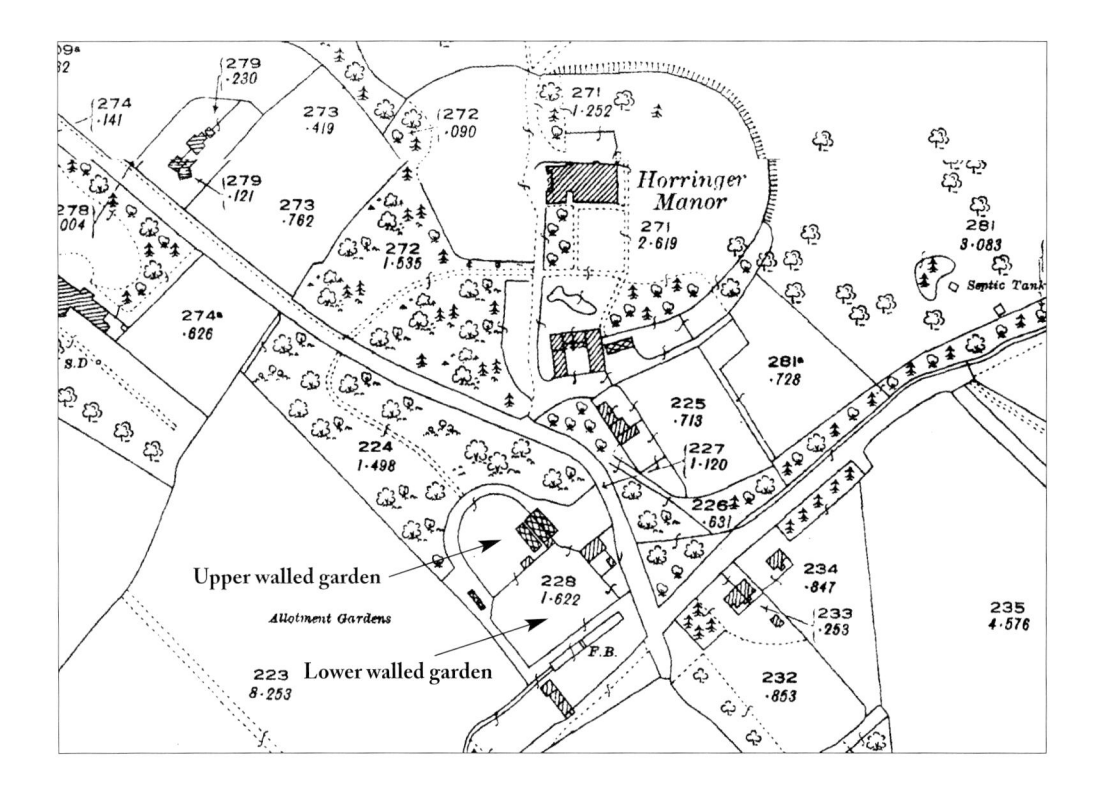

OS 3rd edition map 1926. Courtesy of Ordnance Survey

canalised part of a stream that provide an effective 'drain' to allow frost to flow out of the garden. The middle gate has been replaced, although similar in style to the lower gate on the south-east side. The paths are grassed over, but it is clear there was once a central axis path and one around the perimeter. At a central point in this upper garden, where the paths cross, there is a very pronounced echo effect – was this engineered intentionally or is it a characteristic of many walled gardens?

The lower garden is larger and six sided. On the east side is the former bothy and a single store, built in the cottage orné style – now substantially enlarged – and incorporating the gothic-style pointed archways of the various gates into both gardens. However, the centrally placed gate leading from the garden is ornate wrought iron and the insertion of substantial stone hangers to support the gate furniture is rather more decorative than would have been expected, as is the capping of the main wall in the upper garden that culminates in a castellated course with two tiles. Here the walls are lower and consist of a mixture of brick and flint; one of them has rounded caps without the castellation and tiles. Beyond the lower wall the path continues to a bridge of uncertain age crossing a stream that has been canalised the length of the wall – very similar, but on a smaller scale, to the canal formed by the River Linnet in Ickworth Park.[4] An ornately constructed gully, now bypassed but recently restored, was designed to take the stream to the lower level ditch running parallel to the lane.

The exterior of the garden is of equal interest. The shaded reverse side of the curved wall is an excellent example of the slip system of retarding fruit to produce a crop over a longer period. The remaining espaliered trees were much less vigorous than those on the sunny side of the wall. In the 1970s fruit and vegetables from the walled garden were sold locally in wooden produce boxes labelled 'Horringer Manor'. The remains of a glasshouse on the outer wall contains strawberry boards and evidence that flowers were produced there, notably violas. Backing on to it – but inside the walls – is the sunken boiler house and a boiler that was made by 'C. Smith & Co, Beards Patent, Bury St Edmunds'. It is another reminder of a former local enterprise.[5] Inside the potting shed complex are a considerable number of artefacts and tools, including puffers, burners for fumigators, bee keeping equipment, an old seed drill marker, barn cloches and clips, armatures for floral decorations and various pots.

Today there is scant evidence of cultivation. A few fruit trees and a number of labels detailing the trees and dated 1934 survive. In both gardens there are nail holes in the walls – a record of busier times, when Horringer Manor, like so many estates around Bury St Edmunds, was able to supply the town with its surplus produce, which was particularly important for modestly sized estates such as this.

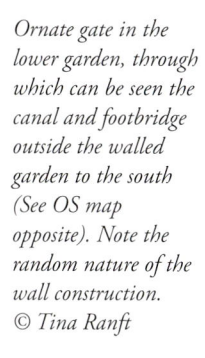

Ornate gate in the lower garden, through which can be seen the canal and footbridge outside the walled garden to the south (See OS map opposite). Note the random nature of the wall construction.
© *Tina Ranft*

Lean-to glasshouse on the outside of the upper garden, showing chimney for the boiler made by C. Smith & Co. The arched doorway to the left gives access into the lower garden.
© *Tina Ranft*

CASE STUDIES: THE WALLED GARDEN, HORRINGER

WOODSIDE, CONSTITUTION HILL, IPSWICH

View from the rear of the the house across the walled garden towards Valley Road.
© J. A. Broster

Less than 10 minutes walk from Christchurch Park, and facing onto Constitution Hill, lies Woodside – an imposing Italianate style mansion set in 4.5 acres (1.82 hectares) of grounds in a fashionable part of Victorian Ipswich. The house, completed in 1872 by 'Mr Eade, Architect' and the local building firm of Cattermole, was built for John Limmer, a prosperous grocer and cheese merchant of the town. It remained in his family until 1900 and was then owned by James Howells, who by 1904 had completed much of the layout of the grounds still largely recognisable today.[1] In 1910 it was bought by the Paul family and stayed in their ownership until 2011.

Constitution Hill runs along a ridge that drops very steeply to Valley Road. The wooded incised ridge effectively forms the third boundary of the walled garden, which is actually bounded by only two walls. The southern and western sides are not walled but formed by the trees and shrubs of the pleasure gardens. The walled garden is clearly visible from Valley Road (A1214), the north ring road of Ipswich, which was constructed in the 1930s on land that was originally part of the property. Miss Paul, the owner of the property until 2011, remembered riding out from the house across open countryside. From Valley Road the garden presents itself as a large and well-maintained urban walled garden on a steeply sloping site. Access to the property is through the main entrance on Constitution Hill and the drive divides – taking guests to the front entrance or down a steep track to the stables. This track forks, with a further track leading to the walled garden.[2]

In 1900 Pear Tree Walk, as this track was named at the time, was planted with almost 500 fruit trees, and the kitchen garden itself had a further 350

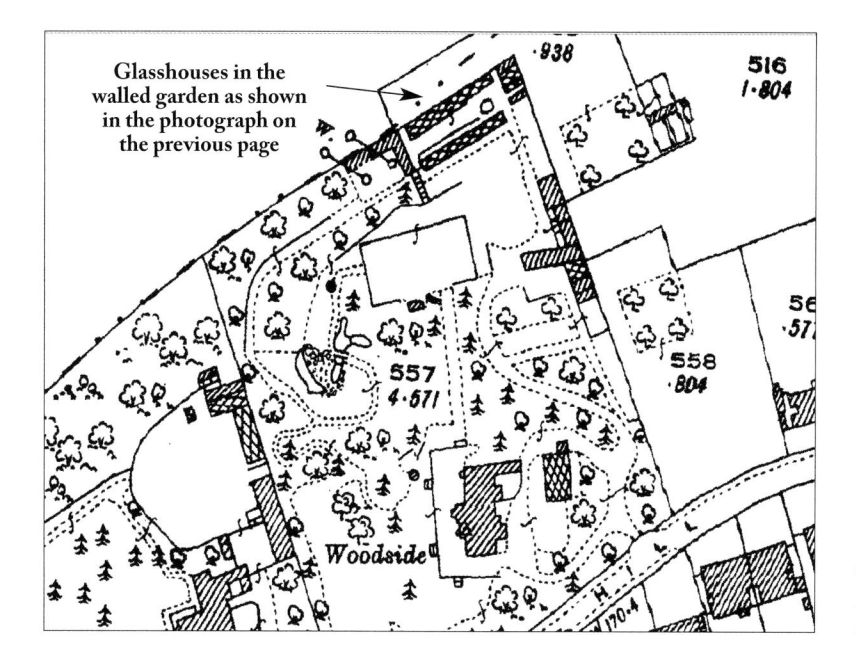

OS 3rd edition map 1927. Courtesy of Ordnance Survey

or more specimens of apples, pear, cherry, plum, walnut, filbert and other nut trees. The substantial ranges of glasshouses housed mostly Alicante and Black Hamburgh vines. There was a large tomato house and additional buildings, including a mushroom house and potting shed.[3] At the time of a visit to the garden in March 2011 there were two fruit stores that would have stored fruit for many months – the quantity of fruit grown in its heyday must have been prodigious.

In 2011 the property was for sale and the walled garden was under-used. However, the garden buildings and artefacts were an impressive reminder of its former days. A walled garden with only two walls is unusual, with one to the north formed by glasshouses and the other to the east. The walls were constructed of high quality brick and buttressed from the outside. There were two parallel rows of glasshouses, one built between 1884 and 1904 and partially demolished, the other positioned adjacent to a store and boiler room. The boiler was manufactured *c.* 1884 by the Norwich firm of Boulton & Paul.[4] The partially demolished range of glasshouses was surrounded by a numerous large and fragrant violets. At the visit, one of the gardeners recalled large quantities of flowers being grown for the house and guests, mentioning in particular violets and carnations.

The first of these surviving glasshouses was a three-quarter-span variety with top opening vents, which hangs off the wall, and like its companion it had impressive ornamental wrought iron supports – although both varied in design. In the second of the two were vines, but according to the gardener, it might formerly have also been used to grow strawberries, and some strawberry boards were found at the time of the visit. All of the

One of the remaining glasshouses in the north-east corner of the garden.
© *J. A. Broster*

A dipping pond within the garden showing one of the many forms of water storage used.
© *J. A. Broster*

heating pipes remained, and in places part of the rope edging around the beds. In front of the glasshouses lay the original dipping pond, now used as an ornamental fishpond. The glasshouses also held a range of galvanised tanks, brick troughs and an underground cistern to collect the run-off from the various glasshouses and buildings. Elsewhere in the garden were further tanks, one with a slate cover to prevent evaporation. The garden had a varied and extensive range of water containers. This, and the numerous cloches and frames, would indicate that the garden must have produced considerable amounts of vegetables as well as fruit.

The adjacent storeroom or potting shed[5] that was well shelved and conveniently placed contained a Crane boiler in the cellar. The shed abutting onto the outer wall of the eastern boundary – accessed through a doorway that led outside to a grassed area – was probably once used for storing hardier vegetables. From here there was a small orchard with a path leading back towards the house. There was no evidence of a bothy, though there was the substantial head gardener's cottage, well outside the garden and probably built in the 1930s. The assumption being that as an urban garden, further accommodation for under gardeners would not have been required.

As well as being a fascinating example of an urban walled garden and one that was developed rather late in the history of walled gardens, Woodside was notable for the huge range of artefacts, pots, and water containers, with cloches being of particular note.

56 WALLED GARDENS OF SUFFOLK

CASE STUDIES: ENDNOTES

ABBOT'S HALL, STOWMARKET
1. SGT (Suffolk Gardens Trust) Survey, Abbot's Hall, April, Oct. 2005.
2. SRO (Suffolk Record Office) (Ipswich) FB221/c.4 1-3, Tithe Map and Apportionment, Stowmarket, 1839; Sale Particulars, Abbot's Hall, 25 June 1858; OS (25 inches to 1 mile), 1st edn. 1885.
3. These were grass fields set aside from at least the fourteenth century for the game of 'camping' or 'camp ball', a cross between football and handball – a particularly East Anglian form of recreation from at least the fourteenth century. It is likely that this area of land became part of Abbot's Hall at a relatively early date, possibly *c.* 1700 at the time of the rebuilding of the hall and development of the formal gardens: D. Dymond, 'Camping Closes', in D. Dymond and E. Martin, *An Historical Atlas of Suffolk* (Ipswich 1995), pp.154–5.
4. OS (25 inches to 1 mile), 3rd edn. 1926.
5. Only some fragments of floor tiles and the brick plant wall now remain of the conservatory shown on OS maps of 1885 and 1926. It formed an integral part of the western end of the walled garden, and its demolition may well have coincided with the planting of the yew hedge that still formed the western side of the garden in 2005.
6. The glasshouse – an extended lean-to – is attached to the inside of the north wall. A plate on the door reads 'Boulton and Paul, Norwich'. It first appears on the 1926 OS map.
7. The potting shed, a wooden lean-to structure with corrugated iron roof, contains a Monad boiler with piping through the wall into the garden. It probably dates from the 1900s, is attached to the outside of the north wall, and appears for the first time on the 1926 OS Map. The summer house in the south-east corner, shown on the maps of 1885 and 1926 has since been demolished.
8. S. Kington, *Report on daffodils seen at Abbot's Hall Stowmarket, on 25 March 2005, prepared for the Museum of East Anglian Life*.
9. *East Anglian Daily Times*, 30 July 2009.

BARTON MERE HOUSE, GREAT BARTON
1. Hodskinson's *Map of Suffolk in 1783* (Dereham, Norfolk 2003).
2. SRO (Bury) PL614//3/18, Pakenham Tithe Map and Award, 1843.
3. SRO (Bury) K513, Photographs, Barton Mere House, March 1975.

LANGHAM HALL
1. A recently discovered eighteenth century map in a private collection reveals that the windows were in fact chutes for the removal of dung and other waste from the adjacent stables, long since demolished, which are now located adjacent to the house. Information ex. Phil Mizen, proprietor of Mizen Herbs, at Walled Kitchen Gardens Forum, Helmingham, Suffolk, 6 Oct. 2012.
2. S RO (Ipswich) HB8/5/5/10, account book of Henry and John Turnor.
3. P. Aitkens and N. Evans, *A History of Langham Hall* (privately printed, 1987), passim.
4. SRO (Bury) HA530/2/34, Estate Map, Langham Hall (1832).
5. SRO (Bury) HA530/1/33, Langham Hall, deeds and papers (Joseph Wilson) 1752–1838.
6. Quoted in T. Williamson, *Suffolk's Gardens & Parks: Designed Landscapes from the Tudors to the Victorians* (Macclesfield, 2000), p. 152.
7. OS map (25 inches to 1 mile) 1st edn. 1884

8. OS map (25 inches to 1 mile) 2nd edn. 1904.
9. In 2012 the property was put up for sale and the future of both the kitchen garden and location of the National Collection of Alpine Campanulas remains uncertain.
10. The Maitland Wilsons were a wealthy Yorkshire family of shipping magnates.

NOWTON COURT, BURY ST EDMUNDS
1. J. Fiske (ed.), *The Oakes Diaries 1778–1827*, Suffolk Records Society, l.XXX11, Pt.1 (Ipswich 1989–91), pp.1–165; T. Williamson (2000), op. cit., pp. 119–20; White, *Directory of Suffolk* (1855), p. 474.
2. SRO (Bury) HA535/5/34, *Plans and Particulars of the Estate of Orbell Ray Oakes Esq at Nowton and Little Whelnetham in the County of Suffolk, J. G Lenny, Surveyor, Bury St Edmunds*, 1832.
3. SRO (Bury) HA5355/5/1-8,10-13, expansion of park, walled garden and other buildings 1876–8. The archive also includes sales catalogues not only by Boyd, but also Renell's *Patent System of Glazing and Plant Houses* and a trade card from James Watts & Co., Horticultural Builders, London.
4. SRO (Bury) HA535/5/7b/8b/11, various specifications regarding building work at Nowton.
5. OS map (25 inches to 1 mile), 1st edn. 1885.
6. Whether or not Bacon's plans were ever fully realised would require more research to correlate extant evidence with the surviving plans, several of which were kindly provided by John Smithson, Parks Development Manager, from the St Edmundsbury Borough Council's archive.
7. J. S., 'Nowton Court' *The Gardener's Chronicle*, II, Nov. 3, 1883, pp. 557–8.

RENDLESHAM HALL
1. W. M. Roberts, *Lost Country Houses of Suffolk* (Woodbridge, 2012), pp. 130–4.
2. White, *Directory of Suffolk* (1844), pp. 201–2; SRO (Ipswich) P461/202, Tithe Map, Rendlesham, 1840.
3. OS map (25 inches to 1 mile), 2nd edn 1887; ibid. 3rd edn 1904; T. B., 'Rendlesham Hall' *The Gardener's Chronicle*, 2, Aug. 1881, pp. 178–9.
4. D. C. Stuart, *Georgian Gardens,* (1979), p. 142.
5. T. B, loc. cit.; SRO (Ipswich) SC335/2 Knight, Frank & Rutley, sale catalogue, The House & Park of the Rendlesham Estate, 27 May 1920, *c.* 900 acres, p. 37 lot 28; ibid., SC242/33, John D. Wood & Co, Richard Bond & Sons, 11 July 1922, The Rendlesham Estate 3.400 acres, lot 6, p. 16.
6. OS map 1:1000, Rendlesham Hall, 2005.
7. SRO (Ipswich), newspaper cuttings, Rendlesham pre- and post-1977; Roberts, op.cit., pp. 133–4.

TENDRING HALL, STOKE-BY-NAYLAND
1. W. M. Roberts, op. cit., pp. 154–7, 205 n. 9 and 10; Soane was paid £659 for his designs of the kitchen garden and stables, part of a total amounting to £19,968; T. Williamson (2000), op. cit., pp. 94–5. George Wyatt, a successful London builder and carpenter was the subcontractor for the brickwork and masonry: G. Darley, *John Soane, An Accidental Romantic* (Newhaven USA & London 1997), pp. 7, 78–9.
2. SRO (Bury) HA 108/10/1, Survey of Tendring Hall (1723).
3. J.S. 'Tendring Hall', *The Gardener's Chronicle,* II, Sept 1879, pp. 363–4, and subsequent quotations below.
4. English Heritage, *Register of Parks and Gardens of Special Historic Interest – Part 39 Suffolk* (2004), n.p.
5. W. M. Roberts, op.cit., pp.156–7. However, a former gardener and gamekeeper

on the estate recalls fruit and vegetables being grown commercially in part of the garden in the 1950s.
6. OS (25 inches to 1 mile), 1st edn 1886.
7. At Glemham House, south facing and in an elevated position, the two acre walled garden was supplied by an equally complex system of wells, pumps and large water tanks: T. Newcomb and J. Gathorne-Hardy, *An Artist In The Garden* (Framlingham, 2012), pp.121–4.
8. Soane was commissioned to design various dairies, lodges and garden buildings in 1782, his earliest commission for a house. Letton Hall, Norfolk followed the next year and then Saxlingham Rectory, Norfolk and further designs for Tendring Hall in 1784: D. Stroud, *The Architecture of Sir John Soane*, (1961), p. 24; H. Colvin, *A Biographical Dictionary of British Architects 1600–1840* (New York & London 1980), pp. 765–72.
9. Loudon, discussing the major importance of water supply to a kitchen garden, approvingly quotes Stephen Switzer, whose work, *An Introduction to a General System of Hydrostatics and Hydraulics*, appeared in 1729, 'It is one of the most essential conveniences of a country-seat and especially useful to kitchen crops; for what use can be made of any ground without it?' Loudon then briefly describes how two Scottish gardens, Lundie House, near Dundee and Castle Semple, Paisley, dealt with similar problems to those at Tendring: J. C. Loudon, *An Encyclopedia of Gardening*, (1834), pp.726–7.

THE WALLED GARDEN, HORRINGER
1. Renamed Horringer Manor in 1901/2.
2. SRO (Bury) T1062, Tithe Map, Horringer.
3. Sale Catalogue, Strutt & Parker with Bidwell's *c.* 1995, lot. 4, 'The Walled Garden And Bungalow, *c.* 2.5 acres, an appropriate size kitchen garden for the original estate of *c.* 49 acres'. A 1998 sale catalogue erroneously refers to the bothy as the gardener's cottage. Information kindly supplied by Mrs J. Emerson 25 April 2006, also additional sales catalogues 1995, 1998 and 1999, generously loaned by the late Mr B. Phillips.
4. OS map (25 inches to 1 mile) 3rd edn. 1926.
5. J. Woods, 'Glasshouse manufacturers in Bury', *Suffolk Gardens Trust Newsletter* 27, Spring 2008, pp. 26–7.

WOODSIDE, CONSTITUTION HILL, IPSWICH
1. Stevens, *Directory of Ipswich* (1885), p. 144; Kelly's *Ipswich* (1906), p. 126; ibid. (1920), p. 119. Woodside was the property of the Paul family from 1950 until its sale in June 2011.
2. There were few significant changes to the layout of the garden after 1904.
3. SRO (Ipswich) Q59, Woolnoth Collection, vol. 190, p. 83, sale catalogue 'Woodside', Robert Bond & Sons, Ipswich, 23 May 1900; *East Anglian Daily Times*, 30 June 2011.
4. Boulton & Paul not only manufactured glasshouses, but also a whole range of garden tools, espalier fencing, garden seats, gates, bridges, lawnmowers, urns and even iron plant labels. Among their more ambitious projects were chapels and infirmeries and even a billiard room, complete with portable table and lavatory: R. Last, 'The Maharajah is well satisfied', *Norfolk Gardens Trust Journal*, Spring 2006, pp. 27–38.
5. Two surviving frames outside the potting shed may have contained some of the original '10 Cool Lights' mentioned in the 1900 sale. On a visit to the garden in 2011 several cloches were found in the potting shed, while the fruit store adjacent to the stables contained a rare example of a Chase cloche.

LIST OF SUFFOLK WALLED GARDENS

Below is a list of Suffolk walled gardens compiled directly from Suffolk Gardens Trust Walled Gardens Recording Group's field work or from other sources. It does not claim to be comprehensive, so if you have any further information on those listed or additional examples we would like to hear from you. It should not be assumed that these gardens are open to the public. Please enquire at your local tourist office for clarification.

PROPERTY	CIVIL PARISH	CONDITION	USE, IF KNOWN	ANY OTHER COMMENTS
Abbot's Hall	Stowmarket	Undergoing restoration	Kitchen garden	Museum of East Anglian Life SGT survey April 2005
Ashe High House	Campsea Ashe	Well maintained	Fruit and vegetables	Kitchen garden under divided ownership SGT survey Feb. 2008
Barton Hall	Great Barton	Only walls of hexagonal garden remain	Site now small housing estate	Art & Crafts head gardener's cottage survives SGT survey Nov. 2011
Barton Mere House	Great Barton	Good	Productive kitchen garden	SGT survey April 2012
Bawdsey Manor	Bawdsey	Poor	Fruit, vegetables and flowers	Designed by Parson, Partridge & Tudway 1886–1908; interesting lemonry SGT survey Oct. 2009
Benacre Hall	Benacre	Good	Productive kitchen garden	SGT survey Nov. 2009
Brent Eleigh Hall	Brent Eleigh	Excellent	Commercial kitchen garden in 2005	Unusual chapel (former bothy?) possibly designed by Lutyens SGT survey Mar. 2007
Chantry Park	Ipswich	Now largely dominated by modern glasshouses and polytunnels	Assorted planting	Ipswich Borough Council Horticultural Department SGT survey Oct. 2011
Chilton Hall	Chilton	Good	Fruit and vegetables	Moat forms 4th boundary of walled garden SGT survey April 2006
[The] Clock House	Cransford	Good	Mainly ornamental	Formerly part of Cransford Hall; largely restored *c.* 2009 SGT survey Oct. 2008
Cobbs Hall	Great Saxham	Good	Walled kitchen garden	Created 2003/4; designed by Dr Richard Soper, built by Tony Dargan, bricklayer
Coney Weston Hall	Coney Weston	Not all walls survive	Orchard, lawns	
Culford Hall	Culford	Now partially walled	Grassed over	Created 1795–8; work of de Carlo, Bury St Edmunds stone mason
Elmhurst Park	Woodbridge	One wall only survives	Bowling green	Public park

PROPERTY	CIVIL PARISH	CONDITION	USE, IF KNOWN	ANY OTHER COMMENTS
Euston Hall	Euston	Large, over c. 2 hectares (4 acres); several walled enclosures Not cultivated	No remains of earlier planting. In 1998 partly given over to fruit, vegetables and sheep grazing	Early 17th century gardener's house
Glemham Hall	Little Glemham	Good	Mainly ornamental	SGT survey Jan./Mar. 2007
Glemham House	Great Glemham	Excellent	Fully productive walled kitchen garden	Shaped like a squashed nine-sided polygon
Great Thurlow Hall	Great Thurlow	Good	Walled kitchen garden	
Haughley House	Haughley	Fair	Productive	SGT survey Nov. 2013
Hawstead Place Farm	Hawstead	Poor	Mid-20th century house and garden built within the walls	Described in 1924 as 'a large kitchen garden and orchard'; now only a large portion of walls survive SGT survey Mar. 2014
Helmingham Hall	Helmingham	Excellent	Productive and ornamental	Layout of paths and beds unchanged since the 16th century; moated
Henstead Hall	Henstead	Derelict	Overgrown	Threat of site redevelopment
Heveningham Hall	Heveningham	Good	Productive and ornamental	Early 18th century, later divided into two compartments by a crinkle-crankle wall; single storey brick bothy of interest
Hintlesham Hall	Hintlesham	Now a car park	Walls remain largely intact	Part of golf complex SGT survey Mar. 2009
Horringer House	Horringer	Good	Fruit and vegetables	SGT survey May/Sept. 2006
Ickworth House	Ickworth	Good; construction dates from c. 1703	Vineyard recently uprooted	The National Trust have begun recreating a traditional kitchen garden (2012)
Ilketshall Hall	Ilketshall St Lawrence	Poor	Only fragments of walling remain	Old walls incorporated into 1960s chicken sheds SGT survey Jan. 2008
Kentwell Hall	Long Melford	Excellent	Fine collection of ancient espaliered fruit trees	Mostly 17th century in layout with modern herb garden and potager
Knodishall Hall	Knodishall	Fair	Grassed with planted borders	SGT survey Nov. 2007
Langham Hall	Langham	Good	Productive and commercial	Interesting walled inner garden; holds National Collection of Alpine Campanulas SGT survey April/May 2008
Livermere Park	Great Livermere			In process of restoration to productive commercial use SGT survey Feb. 2010

PROPERTY	CIVIL PARISH	CONDITION	USE, IF KNOWN	ANY OTHER COMMENTS
Marlesford Hall	Marlesford	Good	Decoratively planted	Interesting glasshouses and artifacts
Nowton Court	Nowton	Good		Unusual free-standing central buildings survive; St Edmundsbury Borough Council's Horticultural Department SGT survey March 2011
[The] Old Rectory	Drinkstone	Unknown in 2013		Under restoration (2005) SGT survey Mar./May 2005
[The] Old Rectory	Grundisburgh	Good	Fruit and vegetables	SGT survey Jan. 2009
Parham Hall	Parham	Excellent	Fully productive	Fine example of crinkle-crankle walling
[The] Place for Plants	East Bergholt	Good	Walls intact	Now used as a nursery
[The] Priory	Stoke by Nayland	Good	Productive glasshouses and ornamental	Frame-yard now a swimming pool
Redisham Hall	Redisham	Excellent	Productive and ornamental	Restoration of glasshouses etc., completed 1994 SGT survey April/July 2009
Rendlesham Hall	Rendlesham	Fair	Under used	Monumental in scale; good eg. of a crinkle-crankle wall SGT survey Dec. 2005
Satis House	Yoxford	Good	Mainly ornamental	East wall crinkle-crankle SGT survey Feb. 2009
Saxham Hall	Great Saxham	Fair	Now farmyard extension with pony paddock and manège	SGT survey Oct. 2010
Shrubland Park	Coddenham	Unknown	Site of former nursery	Probably the work of head gardener William Davidson in the 1840s
Somerleyton Hall	Somerleyton	Good	Productive and ornamental	Paxton designed ridge and furrow lean-to glasshouses on north wall
Sternfield House	Sternfield	Fair	Mainly ornamental	Two Dutch-style glasshouses by Harleys dating from the 1940s or 50s beyond west entrance SGT survey Dec. 2012
Sudbourne Hall	Sudbourne	Derelict	Remains of earlier horticultural use	Sympathetic housing development approved, safeguarding walls (2012). Head gardener's cottage a fine eg. of Arts & Crafts style SGT survey Mar. 2008

PROPERTY	CIVIL PARISH	CONDITION	USE, IF KNOWN	ANY OTHER COMMENTS
Tendring Hall	Stoke-By-Nayland	Derelict	Now used for rearing pheasants	External walls a graceful reminder of Soane's work (1784) SGT survey April 2010
Theberton House	Theberton	Good	Productive	Unusual circular brick fruit store adjacent to garden SGT survey Sept. 2010
Thornham Hall	Thornham Magna	Good	Partly restored by Prof. Thody 1990–2000	Run by a charitable trust for training young people with learning disabilities in horticulture SGT survey May/Sept. 2007
[The] Walled Garden, Benhall	Benhall	Good	A commercial garden centre/nursery	Once part of Benhall Lodge estate; original buildings sensitively restored and adapted SGT survey Dec. 2006
[The] Walled Garden, Horringer	Horringer	Good	Largely ornamental	Once sensitively integrated within the grounds of Horringer Manor, now in separate ownership SGT survey Mar. 2006
Woodside	Constitution Hill, Ipswich	Fair	Now largely ornamental, but original storerooms and glasshouses remain	A fine example of a prosperous Victorian town garden 1874–c. 1904 SGT survey Mar. 2011

GLOSSARY OF WALLED GARDEN TERMS

Axial. In a conventional rectangular walled garden, axial paths quartered the space, which was then further quartered into sixteen beds.

Apiary. Before the advent of sugar, honey was very important and bees featured heavily in the walled garden. Originally housed in **skeps,** often placed for protection in **bee boles,** of course they were very important in the pollination of plants, an old verse records:
'A swarm of bees in May is worth a load of hay,
A swarm of bees in June is worth a silver spoon,
A swarm of bees in July is not worth a fly'

Beavertail glass. Glass panes that are curved on the lower edge. The water runs down the centre of the curved pane, ensuring that the water is thrown away from the wooden glazing bars, minimising rotting.

Bee bole. Found in older walled gardens, a bee bole is an arched niche built into thick walls in which bee skeps were placed. They became redundant with the development of free-standing, waterproof hives. Chilton Hall has two.

Boot scraper. Most head gardeners seem to have been martinets in respect of mud, mud on the paths (see **hoggin** and **edging**) could be a sackable offence! The garden would often feature boot scrapers at the corner of the individual beds as well as at the entrance to buildings.

Bothy. Accommodation for unmarried, junior gardeners. Usually comprising a kitchen/sitting room and one or two bedrooms, generally fairly spartan and cramped and situated adjacent to the boiler room. It was usually the job of a junior gardener to refuel the boiler throughout the night. Very few complete bothies remain in Suffolk, remnants can be seen at Rendlesham, Thornham, Sudbourne and Tendring.

Capping. Found on top of walls to prevent water entering the wall, freezing and blowing the bricks. There are various cappings, ranging from the simplest form of bricks laid on edge across the wall to specially made bricks with an overhang to throw the water off and away from the wall. Similiarly designed stone cappings are often used, particularly on walls visible from the house. Many were simpler, using slate or lead, and some were shaped or bevelled.

Cistern. Used to collect and store rainwater. Originating from the sixteenth century, they were originally made of lead and then slate and latterly caste iron. At Langham a very ingenious version was actually underground and under-cover. Excellent examples of slate water tanks are to be found at Abbot's Hall, Woodside and Tendring.

Cloche. Normally two or four panes of glass with galvanised metal wires holding them together and with a handle for carrying. There is a variety of styles such as tent, barn and lantern cloches.

Conservatory, see Orangery/stove house.

Crinkle-crankle wall. Also called serpentine walls. They were often 45.7 cm (18 inches) thick and up to 91.4 to 122 cm (3 to 4 feet) high. Single brick or skin serpentine wall: the single skin construction was easy and cheap to build and the undulating line gave strength to what otherwise would have been a very unstable construction, though buttresses were often added later. Largely found in East Anglia, particularly Suffolk, fruit trees were planted in the bays, which afforded shelter. This form of wall was often used in the earlier walled gardens. At Rendlesham one can see where it was used to good effect in the older kitchen garden, built before the very sophisticated nineteenth century garden. Also can be seen at Parham Hall.

Dipping pool. Generally these were centrally placed circular pools from which the gardeners could fill their watering cans, and generally quite large so as to collect as much water as possible. On some sites, particularly sloping ones, water was collected from buildings and then fed into the pond. Originally lined with puddled clay, though later ones are concrete lined, as at Sudbourne.

Drip guard, see capping.

Dutch lights. Also known as headlights or lights, these were glazed frames that could be placed over **frames,** affording extra protection for tender plants or plants that were being **forced.** They could be raised during the day to moderate temperature and provide ventilation.

Engine. Cylindrical water tank on wheels, ideal for spraying and watering or administering **liquid manure.**

Edging. Used to delineate the paths that divided the garden into plots and to keep soil off the paths. They can take many forms: hooped wood, willow, iron, brick and stone. More decorative ones in terracotta have patterned tops: saw-toothed, rope-edged or barley-twist. Terracotta is generally glazed. Box was also used for edging, as the roots formed a dense mat to hold back the soil.

Espalier/step-over. Espalier was a fruit tree that was trained horizontally against a wall or free-standing, thinned to a triangular shape and the branches **nailed** or attached to **straining wires**, enabling fruit to ripen more readily. An additional benefit was that the area under the tree could be used for other crops. A **step-over** was, as its name implies, a low-trained, though free-standing, espaliered fruit tree that was used as a decorative edging to plots within the garden.

Fernery. Building that was cool and moist, inside in which ferns were grown. Ferns enjoyed great popularity in the late nineteenth century.

Flue. Either a brick or cast iron chimney stack to take away the smoke at as great a height as possible. They were used in **heated walls** and disguised with a false buttress. The stone cap had a hole to let the smoke out.

Forcing. Any method used to advance fruiting or flowering: **cloches**, **heated walls**, **glasshouses**, **pits** and **frames** were all used to achieve this.

Frame yard. An enclosed area, often outside the walled garden and adjacent to service buildings, where a substantial number of **frames** and **pits** were used for cultivation.

Frost protection. Fruit grown against a wall was often protected against frost by a simple but effective use of long brackets, projecting from the wall at 183 cm (6 feet) centres, usually anchored under the wall's coping. From this straw matting, linen, glass or calico screens were hung. It was said that this could protect against frosts as low as 14 degrees centigrade. When glass was used they were called **glass walls.**

Fruit garden/orchard. A large area outside the walled garden where 'standard' fruit trees were grown, e.g. apples, plums, pears and cherries.

Fruit house. Unheated glass house, usually free-standing, in which fruit trees were grown in pots.

Fruit store. A specifically designed building, often thatched and built against a north wall, to ensure a constant temperature and guard against overheating. Ventilation was crucial and the interior was lined with wood and shelved. Fruit would be laid out not touching on the shelves on a thin layer of sharp sand. A particularly good example is at Glemham Hall. An unusual circular free-standing one is at Theberton. This was outside the walled garden and situated under trees to avoid overheating.

Game larder. A small building with through ventilation, often elevated, in which game was hung. They were often situated adjacent to the walled garden. Examples in Suffolk include Bawdsey Manor and Sudbourne.

Gardener's house/cottage. The head gardener usually had a house of reasonable size and status – generally close to the walled garden. In comparison to the **bothy** for other estate workers, gardener's houses are noticeably larger and more decorative. That at Easton had a veranda and an indoor WC, in comparison to the plain estate cottages and their privies. At Sudbourne and Little Saxham the gardener's cottages are noticeably imposing but, by comparison, that at Langham is modest and built into the walls of the garden, backing onto a glasshouse.

Gardener's tunnel. A tunnel, often taking the form of a pergola, that enabled gardeners to move between different parts of the garden, particularly the ornamental garden, without being seen by the owner or house guests.

Glasshouse, these could be heated or a 'cool house':

Alpine house. After the mid nineteenth century, when mass tourism developed, alpine houses were popular to display alpines brought back from travels in Europe.

Carnation house. Unheated and cool, these houses were the prerogative of the very rich to augment cut flowers from the garden for indoor display.

Fig house. Dedicated to growing more tender forms of figs.

Orchard house. Unheated and free-standing, the glasshouse was used to grow fruit trees in pots so as to get an earlier crop. The trees were often in the same pot for many years.

Orchid house. Similar to carnation houses, though heated, orchid houses provided flowers for button holes and internal displays

Vine house/vinery. For growing dessert grapes. Vines were often planted outside and their stems threaded through the brick plinth.

Heated wall/ Flue wall. A system of heating a wall to protect or advance the growth of a fruit crop. The walls were built so that the heat moved horizontally through the walls upwards. This was achieved by missing out bricks, or the use of slates to support the bricks, thus ensuring that smoke finally exited through the flue.

Hedge. A living plant grown to form a barrier or divide parts of the garden, or used as a backdrop of a border. It can be used to form a recess for statues, provide shelter or with viewing areas cut out as a feature. At Abbot's Hall a hedge forms the fourth wall of the walled garden.

Hoggin. A type of compactable gravel, sometimes containing clay to aid compactability, which was widely used for paths. It degraded if too much mud was left on it, so for this reason **edgings** were used to prevent soil getting onto the paths and there were **boot scrapers**, to ensure that gardeners cleaned soil off their boots rather than dropping it on the paths.

Horticultural show. Horticultural shows were very popular in the nineteenth century and enabled a head gardener to show off his produce. They were also a valuable forum to exchange ideas and knowledge. Prize certificates dating from the 1870s to the 1950s still exist in many Suffolk walled gardens.

Hot bed. Not to be confused with pineapple and melon pits, a hot bed could be created in the vegetable garden or frame yard to produce salad or an early forced crop. A mixture of hot, new horse manure is covered with soil and a frame is placed over it.

Hot house, see glasshouse.

Liquid manure. Often from stable yard or comfrey, but other more complex recipes are widely quoted involving steeping deer dung, chicken manure, soot and often adding quick lime. All was stirred for a number of days and when it was finally clear further diluted before being used on plants in vigorous growth or in bloom, an **engine** was frequently used for this.

Melon/pineapple pit. A glasshouse sunk in the ground and entered down steps, with staging on which melons were grown and trained up the roof and eaves.

Nailing. Before the introduction of **straining wires, espaliers** were often trained by nailing the branches back to the walls. Additionally, fruit was nailed back to support it and the fruit protected from damage by a pad of leather or calico between it and the wall.

Netting fruit. Used widely to prevent fruit falling off and bruising, and still practised today.

Plunging. Planting plants in pots in display beds, or to conceal where crops had finished. The pots were dug in below the surface of the soil and could be changed when they were over their best. For the wealthy this enabled them to always have a pristine display.

Pump. Introduced in the early nineteenth century to augment **cisterns** and **dipping ponds** as a source of water. Generally situated at strategic points in the garden, as at Great Saxham where there were four and a good source of water, as opposed to the pumps at Langham that were situated over a well and above an underground cistern.

Skep. The oldest form of housing hives of bees. Circular in form, they are made of coils of rope. Unlike the later beehive that were waterproof, skeps needed to have a degree of protection and were kept in **bee boles.**

Slip culture/slip garden. The area gardened outside the walled garden, often used for invasive or space-consuming vegetables such as Jerusalem artichokes, pulses and potatoes. In the case of fruit, trees were often grown against the north wall to retard the growth of fruit and extend the season.

Straining wires. Straining wires replaced **nailing** in the late-nineteenth century as a means of training espaliers and supporting fruit. Brackets were fixed to walls, with a hole in the brackets some 6 inches (15 cm) away from the wall at approximately 3 feet (91 cm) centres, through which wire was threaded and strained tight at the end of the wall. It avoided the damaging effect of nailing into the bricks and mortar, and meant that espaliers could be trained more consistently, and that the fruit would not be damaged by contact with the wall.

Strawberry boards. Lengths of planking, suspended inside glasshouses, on which pots of strawberries would be placed to force fruiting and keep the fruit clean. Examples are at Horringer Manor and Woodside.

Vine border. An area in **vine houses,** under the spread of the vines, where early salad crops could be grown.

Winding gear. A series of racks and pulleys that enabled ventilation panels to be raised and lowered in **glasshouses.**

SELECT BIBLIOGRAPHY

Books are published in London unless otherwise stated.

UNPUBLISHED SOURCES

Babergh District Council B/08/01067, P. Aitkens, *The Kitchen Gardens to Woolverstone Hall, now Doubles Nursery, Ipswich: A Report on the Historic Buildings and their Context*, Oct. 2005.

Broster, J. A., *Suffolk Walled Kitchen Gardens*, Dissertation for the BA Arts (Hons.) Degree in History, University of East Anglia and University of Essex, at University Campus, Suffolk, 2009.

Kington, S., *Report on daffodils seen at Abbot's Hall Stowmarket, on 25 March 2005, prepared for the Museum of East Anglian Life*.

Suffolk Gardens Trust, Walled Gardens Group, Surveys and Reports 2005–2013

BOOKS

Brunskill, R. W., *Brick Building in Britain* (1997).

Campbell, S., *Charleston Kedding. A History of Kitchen Gardening* (1996).

Campbell, S., *Walled Kitchen Gardens* (Princes Risborough, 2002).

Campbell, S., *A History of Kitchen Gardening* (2005).

Carter, T., *The Victorian Garden* (1988).

Colvin, H., *A Biographical Dictionary of British Architects 1600–1840* (New York & London, 1980).

Desmond, R., *Bibliography of British Gardens* (Winchester, 1984).

Dymond, D., and Martin E., (eds), *An Historical Atlas of Suffolk* (Ipswich, 1995).

Dymond, D and Northeast P., *A History of Suffolk* (Chichester, 1995).

Fairclough J. and Hardy, M., *Thornham and the Waveney Valley: an historic landscape explored* (Kings Lynn, 2004).

Geddes-Brown, L., *The Walled Garden* (2007).

Grant, F., and Patton J., (eds), *The Walled Gardens of Herefordshire* (Little Logiston, Woonton Almeley, Herefordshire, 2009).

Grant, F., *Glasshouses* (Botley, Oxford, 2013).

Hall, L. (ed.), *Staffordshire Walled Kitchen Gardens* (Codsall, Staffordshire, 2003).

Hobhouse, P., *The Story of Gardening* (2002).

Iredale D., and Barrett J., *Discovering Your Old House* (Princes Risborough, 1997).

Kelleher S., (ed.), *Diary of a Victorian Gardener, William Cresswell and Audley End* (Swindon, 2006).

Morgan J. and Richards, A., *A Paradise out of a Common Field; The Pleasure And Plenty Of The Victorian Garden* (1990).

Musgrave, T., *The Head Gardeners, Forgotten Heroes of Horticulture* (2007).

Newcomb, T. and Gathorne-Hardy, J., *An Artist In The Garden* (Framlingham, 2012).

Paine C. (ed.), *The Culford Estate 1780–1935* (Lavenham, 1993).

Roberts, W., *Lost Country Houses Of Suffolk* (Woodbridge, 2010).

Rutherford, S., with Lovie J., *Georgian Garden Buildings* (Botley, Oxford, 2012).

Sales, J., *Rooted in History, Studies in Garden Conservation* (2001).

Scarfe, N., *Suffolk, A Shell Guide* (1960).
Scarfe N., (ed. and translator), *A Frenchman's Year In Suffolk: French Impressions of Suffolk life in 1784,* Suffolk Records Society, XXX (Woodbridge, 1988).
Smit., M, *The Lost Gardens of Heligan* (2000).
Staff of Heligan Gardens Ltd (ed.), *The Lost Gardens of Heligan, Handbook and Essential Guide to the Gardens & Wider Estate* (St Austell, 2002).
Stuart, D., *Georgian Gardens* (1979).
Tennyson, J., *Suffolk Scene* (London & Glasgow, 1939).
Thacker, C., *The Genius of Gardening, the History of Gardens in Britain and Ireland* (1994).
Williamson, T., *The Landscape of Shrubland Park, A Short History* (Clare, Suffolk, 1997).
Williamson T., *Polite Landscapes Gardens & Society in Eighteenth Century England* (Stroud, 1998).
Williamson T., *Suffolk's Gardens & Parks, Designed Landscapes from the Tudors to the Victorians* (Macclesfield, 2000).
Wilson, C. A. (ed.), *The Country House Kitchen Garden 1600–1950* (Stroud, 1998).

ARTICLES AND PAMPHLETS

Auston K., 'Another Brick in the Wall? Restoration or Decay: The State of Walled Gardens in Devon Today', *The Devon Gardens Trust Journal*, l, 1 Sept. 2008, pp. 8–11.
'T.B.' 'Rendlesham Hall', *The Gardener's Chronicle*, 2, Aug. 1881, pp. 178–9.
Bray P., 'Oxburgh Hall Gardens', *Norfolk Gardens Trust Journal*, 13, Autumn 2011, pp. 11–12.
Burns, P., Crinkle-Crankle Walls, Suffolk Gardens Trust newsletter, 22, Autumn 2005, pp. 8–9.
Cox A., Lowther D., Nuttall R., & Styles P., *The Walled Kitchen Garden At Copped Hall And The Story Of Its Restoration* (The Copped Hall Trust, Feb. 2011).
Gregory S., 'Vegetables For The Kitchen Garden', *Staffordshire Gardens and Parks Newsletter*, 21, March 2000, n.p.
Haynes S., 'The Kitchen Garden At Enville House', *Staffordshire Walled Kitchen Gardens* (Codsall, 2003), p. 40.
Last R., 'The Maharajah is well satisfied', *Norfolk Gardens Trust Journal*, Spring 2006, pp. 27–38.
Last R., 'Hoveton Hall – Glasshouse Restoration', *Norfolk Gardens Trust News*, 12, Autumn 2010, pp. 9–10.
Martin E., 'Where are all the Crinkle-Crankle Walls?', *Suffolk Gardens Trust Newsletter*, 30, Autumn 2009, p. 23.
Paul A., 'Tools of the Trade', *Suffolk Gardens Trust Newsletter*, 26, Autumn 2007, p. 24.
Paul A., 'Protected Cropping', *Suffolk Gardens Trust Newsletter*, 34, Autumn 2011, pp. 18–19.
'J.S.', 'Tendring Hall', *The Gardener's Chronicle, II,* Sept. 1879, pp. 363–4.
Scriven P., 'The Primrose Parson', *Suffolk Gardens Trust Newsletter*, 28, Autumn 2008, p. 10.
Springett P. F., 'Westbury in Suffolk? Or the Lost Gardens of Ashe High House', *Garden History,* V, Summer 1974, 2, No. 3, pp. 77–89.
Surry N., 'A Suffolk Heligan or a Future for Walled Kitchen Gardens', *Suffolk Gardens Trust Newsletter*, 33, Spring 2011, pp. 4–6.
Wilcox A., 'The Gardens of Sir Thomas Gooch, Bart.', *Garden Life,* 2, Oct. 1879, pp. 9–11.
Woods J., 'Glasshouse Manufacturers in Bury', *Suffolk Gardens Trust Newsletter*, 27, Spring 2008, pp. 26–7.